MW00851788

WILHELMINA AMARA

BONUS INSIDE

Lost
Native American
Herbalist's
SECRETS

REDISCOVER THE FORGOTTEN POWER OF
150+ TRANSFORMATIVE HERBS

ALL IN 1

Build Your Own Healing Garden and Use Ancient
Herbal Practices for Modern Living

© **Copyright 2024 - All rights reserved.**

The content contained within this book may not be reproduced, duplicated, or transmitted without direct written permission from the author or the publisher.

Under no circumstances will any blame or legal responsibility be held against the publisher or author for any damages, reparation, or monetary loss due to the information contained within this book, either directly or indirectly.

Legal Notice:

This book is copyright-protected. It is only for personal use. You cannot amend, distribute, sell, use, quote, or paraphrase any part of this book's content without the author's or publisher's consent.

Disclaimer Notice:

Please note that the information contained within this document is for educational and entertainment purposes only. All effort has been executed to present accurate, up-to-date, reliable, and complete information. No warranties of any kind are declared or implied. Readers acknowledge that the author is not engaged in rendering legal, financial, medical, or professional advice. The content within this book has been derived from various sources. Please consult a licensed professional before attempting any techniques outlined in this book.

By reading this document, the reader agrees that under no circumstances is the author responsible for any direct or indirect losses incurred because of the use of the information contained within this document, including, but not limited to, errors, omissions, or inaccuracies.

Table of Contents

Introduction

Modern life comes with constant noise and demands. Everywhere you turn, phones are ringing, cars are honking, and distractions are demanding your attention. With a lot of things happening, stress comes, leaving you stuck in a cycle of reaching for over-the-counter pills for the slightest discomfort, losing touch with the natural ways to heal and maintain health. Think about it. *When was the last time you felt truly well—free from illness but full of vitality and a deep sense of peace?*

With the world changing at an unprecedented pace, you cannot afford to live disconnected lives any longer. The time to reclaim your health and your connection to nature is now. Native American Herbalism, a realm deep in tradition, promising physical cures and a path to reforge your spiritual bond with nature, will help you do so.

Perhaps you might think, *"Can this make a difference in my life?"* Yes—it will. As someone fortunate to walk this path, Native American Herbalism illuminates the natural healing and holistic well-being within me. All these experiences and passion prompt the creation of this book that advocates for holistic health and alternative healing. Through Native American Herbalism, learn 33 techniques, tips, and strategies for herbal remedies, ranging from 150+ herbs that soothe a headache to those that calm your mind and lift your spirit.

Beyond the list of plants and their uses, this book will be your one-stop guide to reconnecting with nature, understanding its rhythms, and finding a way to live in harmony. By the time you reach the last chapter, you will be equipped with the knowledge to foster physical wellness and learn the tools for a transformative spiritual transformation.

CHAPTER 1

Origins of Native American Herbalism

Herbal medicine has deep roots in Native American culture, intertwined with their connection to nature. Explore the origins, beliefs, and practices that form the foundation of Native American herbalism in the first chapter.

Discover how Native American tribes developed a vast knowledge of using plants for healing through careful observation and intuition. Learning so fosters a deep respect for the plants used in herbal preparations. The chapter also presents herb categories, from tall trees to tiny ferns. Finally, observe how these ancient practices have evolved and influenced modern medicine.

Roots of Herbal Practices

When thinking of herbal medicine, the image that often comes to mind is modern herbal supplements or age-old remedies from far-off places. Yet, right in the heart of North America, the Native American communities have been practicing herbalism for thousands of years.

Origins and Significance

Centuries ago, no convenience stores, pharmacies, or doctors with modern tools existed. But illnesses existed, as did remedies. The diverse landscapes of North America provided many natural resources for Native American tribes, including medicinal plants. Through careful observation of the natural world for generations, traditional ecological knowledge was developed.

Such knowledge enabled them to identify herbs and other plants with healing properties. These practices were not random trial and error but founded on deep understanding, cultivation, and sustainable harvesting. The tribes observed which plants animals consumed to self-medicate. This process is known as *zoopharmacognosy* and helps identify potential medicinal uses of plants.

For instance, indigenous peoples in Peru observed that parrots ate clay from riverbanks, likely as an antidote to toxins in their diet. This ethnozoological knowledge led them to experiment with medicinal clays to treat poisoning and upset stomachs in people. They intuited that the clays bound to toxins and absorbed harmful compounds based on the geophagy behaviors of parrots. The careful attention to the interaction between animals and the environment enabled them to identify and utilize the medicinal properties of clays. Through respectful relationships with plants as living beings and guided by ancestral wisdom, Native Americans developed holistic systems of herbal medicine.

Prominent Herbal Tribes

Tribes that contributed to the annals of Native American Herbalism are listed as follows:

The Cherokee

The Cherokee people possess practices intertwined with the tribe's history. *"Nvwoti,"* which suggests that plants are not just organisms but kindred spirits with a unique life force, is the foundation of their beliefs. When Cherokee healers collect plants for medicinal purposes, they do so with reverence, often saying prayers to acknowledge the plant's life. Physical symptoms and spiritual aspects were considered in diagnosing ailments—the goal of the Cherokee is to bring the body, mind, and spirit into a harmonious state.

Various native plants form the foundation of Cherokee nutrition and medicine. Among these herbs are ginseng, black cohosh, bloodroot, and spicebush. Cherokee healers are adept at spotting these plants in their natural habitats and know how to transform them into teas, tinctures, balms, and other medicinal concoctions.

Knowledge about these herbs and healing techniques is an oral tradition passed down from generation to generation. Historically, aspiring healers went through rigorous training to master their craft. Today, this wisdom is not confined to oral tales; it is also preserved in books, courses, and apprenticeship programs that welcome Cherokee and non-Cherokee learners.

The Navajo

Being long intertwined with the land, the Navajo people, known as Diné, respect nature and understand that humans are intimately connected to the world around them. The Navajo believe that plants, like humans, possess spirits and are living beings with whom one can communicate and collaborate. For them, every herb has its purpose, and collecting them is a sacred ritual. Ceremonies and prayers were offered as Navajo healers source plants, ensuring the act was done with gratitude and mindfulness.

The Iroquois

The Iroquois, also known as the Haudenosaunee or Six Nations, are a confederation of Native American tribes renowned for their political innovations and rich cultural traditions. Among their many practices, the herbal traditions of the Iroquois stand out, showcasing the tribe's relationship with the natural world.

Drawing upon the bounties of the land, the Iroquois have a vast knowledge of the medicinal, nutritional, and spiritual significance of plants and herbs. Rooted in the belief that every plant carries a spirit and purpose, Iroquois herbalists treat plants with deep respect, often engaging in ceremonies and offering thanks before harvesting.

Aside from being remedies for physical ailments, the herbal practices of the Iroquois extend to spiritual aiding. For example, plants like sweetgrass, sage, and cedar are not only used for physical healing but also for purification and spiritual upliftment.

Core Spiritual Beliefs

Every practice or tradition is rooted in certain principles and beliefs that guide its essence.

Everything Has a Spirit

Behind the tangible practices of herbal medicine lie the intangible beliefs that truly form its soul. Among Native American tribes, spiritual beliefs bind together their everyday actions and cosmic understanding. Central to this is the principle that everything has a spirit. *But what does this truly mean, and how does it influence the Native American approach to herbalism?*

To truly comprehend the Native American worldview, imagine a world where everything pulsates with life. Not just animals or humans but every rock, stream, and gust of wind. Such a deep-seated belief infuses every interaction of each tribe with sanctity.

Also, *have you ever felt the serenity of a sunrise or the melancholy of a lone tree atop a hill?* To the Native American tribes, such feelings are communications. The sunrise might be sharing the joy of a new beginning, and the tree might be reminiscing tales of yesteryears. Every rustle of leaves, every ripple in the water is nature conversing if only one listens.

Mutual Respect

In many cultures, nature is often viewed through a utilitarian lens: *what can it provide,* or *how can it be used?* But the dynamics change when you believe every herb or plant has a spirit. It is no longer about extraction but about coexistence. The plants become more than resources.

Harvesting a plant for medicinal purposes is thus a sacred one. The healer or gatherer often starts with silence, acknowledging the plant's presence. Softly uttered prayer or song, asking for permission, was also offered. Once the herb is harvested, a word or gesture of gratitude is expressed, sometimes even leaving behind a small offering. This ritual ensures that the act remains grounded in humility and respect.

Holistic Approach to Health

In the modern world, health is often reduced to numbers— weight, blood pressure, or cholesterol levels. But in the Native American worldview, health is more about physical, mental, and spiritual well-being. Imagine a tripod where each leg represents one of these aspects. If one leg weakens or is shorter, the entire structure becomes unstable—the Native Americans see health that way.

Anxiety, restlessness, or spiritual disconnection might not show up on any medical test, yet they are as indicative of health *(or the lack thereof)* as a fever or a wound. To the Native American tribes, these non-physical symptoms are messages and signals from the body and spirit indicating an imbalance or disharmony.

Healing as Restoration

If health is a balanced state of being, healing is the art of restoring this balance. Instead of silencing the symptoms, the root cause was addressed, harmonizing the dissonant notes. In this holistic view, a headache might not just be treated with a herb for pain relief but also with a ritual to calm a restless spirit or a chant to soothe an agitated mind.

When you approach illness in this holistic manner, the options for healing expand. Herbs, with tangible properties, address physical ailments. Rituals, on the other hand, serve as therapeutic practices to align the spirit to reestablish your connection with nature and the cosmos. Chants act as meditative tools, calming the mind and bringing mental clarity. Together, the two create a healing regimen that looks beyond the manifest symptoms, aiming to rejuvenate the individual at every level.

Nature as a Teacher

Native American tribes see nature as a living library filled with wisdom in its raw, unadulterated form. Observing a deer nibbling on a particular herb when it seemed agitated or a bird choosing a specific plant after a strenuous flight was not a mere coincidence to them. These were clues, lessons in natural medicine offered freely by the universe.

Why do animals do what they do? To the Native American tribes, the behaviors were imbued with deep wisdom. As a part of nature, animals inherently understood its rhythms and remedies. By observing and mimicking these patterns, tribes could harness this wisdom. For example, when a bear is seen consuming certain berries before hibernation, it might indicate the berries' nutritional or medicinal potency in preparing the body for long rest periods.

Interconnectedness

In the eyes of Native American tribes, every entity—*human, animal, plant, or inanimate object*—is a part of this web of existence. To truly understand interconnectedness, consider the ripple effect in a pond. A single pebble dropped into the water creates waves that impact the entire surface. Similarly, when you grasp the concept of interconnectedness, you realize that every action has consequences, no matter how small. A tree felled or a river polluted does not just affect the immediate vicinity. The repercussions are felt throughout the ecosystem and, by extension, every being part of it. Your health, spirit, and essence are intertwined with the health and spirit of the world around you.

Balance

Predators and prey, night and day, seasons and cycles — everything works in tandem, ensuring the harmony of existence. From the Native American perspective, physical, mental, or spiritual ailments are disruptions in this harmony.

In this context, herbal remedies serve as realignment tools, instruments to mend the disrupted chords of existence. Native American healers administer an herb to restore the balance, mending the cosmic web where the disruption occurred. It might be the body being brought back to health, the spirit being soothed, or the mind finding clarity. The goal is always holistic healing—reestablishing the individual's place in the grand symphony of life.

Tradition Meets Modernity

Like a river carving its path through millennia, Native American herbalism has transformed, too. In the early days, Native American herbal practices were deeply intertwined with spiritual rituals. Ceremonies marked the harvest of herbs, and chants and dances often accompanied their use. Over time, while the spiritual connection remained robust, these practices also began to address everyday health needs. What began as sacred rituals for specific occasions transitioned into daily wellness routines.

As tribes migrated or the environment changed, so did their herbal practices. New plants were discovered, and old ones were left behind. This fluidity allowed Native American herbalism to remain relevant, ensuring that the knowledge passed down through generations remained rich and adaptive.

Influence on Modern Medicine

Do you know where aspirin, a common household medicine, originates from? Aspirin is derived from the willow tree, a remedy Native Americans use for pain and fever. Many plants central to Native American herbalism have found their way into modern pharmaceuticals, proving that ancient wisdom can complement cutting-edge science.

Challenges in Contemporary Times

As tradition meets modernity, several hurdles arise, demanding reverence for the past and adaptability for the present.

- **Cultural Appropriation vs. Appreciation**: As global interest in Native American herbalism grows, ensure that this knowledge is shared with respect and not commodified or misrepresented.
- **Balancing Tradition and Science**: While many Native American herbal remedies have proven effective over generations, they sometimes lack the empirical evidence modern medicine demands. Bridging this gap requires a collaborative approach, ensuring that tradition is not overshadowed by science and vice versa.
- **Sustainability Concerns**: With rising popularity comes increased demand. Ensure that plants central to Native American herbalism are harvested sustainably. Over-harvesting could deplete resources and disrupt the delicate balance of ecosystems.

Herbs at a Glance

North America's vast landscapes, diverse ecosystems, and the wisdom of Native American tribes have showcased unique plant species. Each category of these plants—*the towering trees or the humble grasses*—carries distinct characteristics that set them apart.

Trees and Shrubs

The commanding presence of trees and the dense growth of shrubs form a significant part of North America's vegetation. Trees and shrubs are usually perennial, living for several years. While trees often stand tall, dominating the landscapes, shrubs are shorter, bushier, and sometimes thorny. Being able to thrive in varied conditions makes them both a shelter and a source of remedies.

Examples:

- **Oak's Strength**: Have deeply rooted systems that offer astringent properties derived from their bark and acorns.
- **Versatile Hawthorn**: A thorny shrub, hawthorn's berries, leaves, and flowers have been used for heart-related conditions.

Wildflowers and Weeds

Wildflowers often grow in specific conditions or seasons, gracing fields, forests, and meadows. Weeds, on the other hand, are hardy survivors, thriving where others might struggle.

Examples:

- **Echinacea's Allure:** Its stunning purple petals boost the immune system.
- **Dandelion's Persistence:** Often labeled as *a 'weed,'* every part of the dandelion, from its roots to its sunny petals, has therapeutic benefits, particularly for liver health.

Grasses and Ferns

Grasses are usually slender, flexible, and hollow-stemmed, thriving in open spaces and often overlooked for their medicinal properties. Ferns, with their feather-like fronds, prefer shade and dampness. Both represent some of the oldest plant forms on Earth.

Examples:

- **Lemongrass's Aroma:** A tall perennial grass that is aromatic and good for digestion and calming nerves.
- **Horsetail Fern's Resilience:** Despite its delicate appearance, horsetail has been used for its diuretic properties and to strengthen bones.

CHAPTER 2

Crafting Native Herbal Remedies

Herbal medicine has been an integral part of Native American culture for centuries. Tribes across North America have leveraged and perfected the art of crafting plant-based remedies that promote body, mind, and spirit well-being. This chapter will guide you through the meticulous extraction methods, combination principles, diverse applications, and profound ritualistic uses that make this tradition so powerful.

Extraction Techniques

Creating herbal remedies requires specific methods of extracting the beneficial properties from plants. These methods, perfected over time, are the backbone of herbal medicine:

Tinctures and Teas

Tinctures and teas are among the oldest methods of herbal extraction. These two are primary ways to consume the goodness of herbs, turning simple plants into potent medicinal concoctions.

Tinctures

A tincture is a concentrated liquid extraction of an herb. The process involves soaking plant material in alcohol or vinegar for several weeks. This method effectively draws out the active components of the herb. The plant material is strained once the soaking period ends, leaving a potent liquid.

Materials:

- Fresh or dried herb of your choice
- High-proof alcohol *(like vodka)* or apple cider vinegar
- Glass jar with a tight-fitting lid
- Strainer

Steps:

1. Fill the glass jar halfway with the herb.
2. Pour the alcohol or vinegar over the herb until it is fully submerged.
3. Seal the jar tightly and store it in a cool, dark place.
4. Shake the jar once a day for about four weeks.
5. After four weeks, strain out the plant material. Store the liquid tincture in a dark glass bottle, preferably with a dropper.

Teas

Herbal teas are perhaps the most familiar method of extraction. It is as simple as steeping dried or fresh herbs in hot water. The heat from the water extracts the plant's helpful compounds, infusing them into the liquid.

Materials:

- Fresh or dried herb of your choice
- Boiling water
- Teapot or mug
- Strainer

Steps:

1. Place the herbs in the teapot or mug. Use one tablespoon of dried or two tablespoons of fresh herbs for a standard serving.
2. Pour boiling water over the herbs.
3. Cover and steep for about 10 to 15 minutes.
4. Strain out the herbs.

Salves and Ointments

When you think of external herbal applications, salves and ointments come to mind. These two have healing, soothing, or protective qualities.

Salves

Salves are a combination of infused herbal oils and beeswax, creating a semi-solid end product.

Materials:

- Fresh or dried herb
- Carrier oil *(like olive oil or coconut oil)*
- Beeswax pellets
- Double boiler or two pots

- Glass jar for storage
- Strainer

Steps:

1. Place your herb and carrier oil in the double boiler. Use about one cup of herb for every cup of oil.
2. Gently heat the mixture on low for 2 to 3 hours, ensuring it does not boil.
3. Strain out the herb, leaving just the infused oil.
4. In the same double boiler, melt one ounce of beeswax for every cup of infused oil.
5. Once melted, combine the beeswax and oil, stirring well.
6. Pour the mixture into glass jars and let it cool.

Ointments

Ointments are similar to salves but typically have a higher oil concentration, making them softer and more spreadable. Particularly, ointments help with conditions that require deep moisturization. To make ointments, follow the same steps as for the salve, but use more infused oil and less beeswax to achieve a softer consistency.

Safety First

Approach nature with respect and knowledge. To do so—

- **Research**: Before using any herb, research its properties, potential side effects, and contraindications. Remember, not all herbs are safe for everyone, especially pregnant or nursing individuals, children, or those with specific medical conditions.

- **Quality Matters:** Ensure that your herbs are free from pesticides and contaminants. Sourcing from reputable suppliers or growing your herbs can significantly affect the quality and efficacy of your remedies.
- **Less is More:** With herbal remedies, starting with a small amount and observing how your body reacts is often better. This way, you can determine the best dosage or application for you.
- **Consultation:** Ask an expert if you are uncertain about an herb or its effects.

Combining Herbs

Herbalists craft potent remedies by combining different herbs. Combining herbs is an art as much as a science, ensuring the blend is effective, harmonious, and safe.

Principles of Mixing

When blending herbs, imagine yourself as an artist with a palette of colors. Each herb offers a unique shade, and your task is to mix these colors to create a harmonious masterpiece. Understand the herb's nature and consider how it interacts with others.

Synergy

Herbs, when combined correctly, can amplify each other's benefits. For instance, if one herb helps with digestion and another calms inflammation, such a combination might aid digestion, reduce inflammation, and boost gut health.

Balance

In herbs, each comes with its own *'energy'* or *'character.'* Some herbs are known to warm, boost circulation, and generate heat within the body. Others might be cooling, providing a soothing effect. Then there are herbs that are drying, perfect for conditions of excess moisture, while some are moistening, beneficial for dry conditions.

Understanding these characters. As such, pick a cooling herb when someone has excessive heat signs, like inflammation or fever. A warming herb can also be incorporated to get its other benefits—just mix it in a way that the product is harmonized.

Support

In any great story, there is a protagonist, and then there is a supporting cast. The same can be applied to herbs. Often, one herb stands out as the primary remedy, addressing the core issue. But, to make the remedy more effective or to mitigate any strong effects of the primary herb, other herbs are added as supporters.

For instance, add chamomile if you are crafting a sleep aid using valerian as the primary herb *(due to its soothing properties)*. Not only does chamomile enhance the calming effects, but it also helps counter any intense effects of valerian, ensuring a peaceful sleep without grogginess.

Taste and Aroma

While the medicinal properties of herbs are essential, so are the taste and aroma, especially when crafting consumables like teas or tinctures. The sensory experience plays a role in the healing process. A remedy that is pleasant to taste and smell is more likely to be consumed regularly, ensuring its benefits are fully reaped.

Consider, for example, the sharp taste of some immune-boosting herbs. While effective, they might be off-putting to some. But when combined with sweet or aromatic herbs like licorice or lavender, the remedy becomes delightful.

Popular Herb Combinations

Some of the common herb combinations that have stood the test of time are the following:

Echinacea and Elderberry

Echinacea boosts immunity, making the body more resilient to illnesses. Elderberry, containing antioxidants and vitamins, supports this immune-boosting activity and offers additional protection against viruses. Together, they create a protective shield for the body, strengthening its natural defenses.

Lemon Balm and Mint

Lemon balm has calming properties that can alleviate stress and anxiety, while mint provides a refreshing zing that revitalizes the senses. These two create a calming brew perfect for relaxation and mental clarity.

Nettle and Dandelion

Nettle, a nutritional powerhouse, is rich in essential nutrients that fortify the body. Dandelion complements this by detoxifying, cleansing the liver, and improving digestive health. Together, these herbs create a nutrient-dense and cleansing tonic that is as refreshing as it is healthful.

Ginger and Yarrow

Ginger, renowned for its spicy kick and digestive benefits, finds a perfect partner in yarrow, known for its anti-inflammatory and wound-healing properties. When used together, they form a therapeutic concoction ideal for those seeking relief from inflammation and digestive discomfort.

Avoiding Harmful Combinations

Herbs are natural, but that does not always mean they are harmless. Much like how certain foods can interact in our body, herbs can, too. While some herbs complement each other beautifully, others might not get along, leading to less-than-ideal outcomes. Below are a few essential guidelines to ensure your herbal mixtures remain beneficial and safe.

Know Each Herb

Imagine herbs as characters in a book. To create a great story, you need to understand each character's background, motivations, and quirks. Similarly, know its unique profile before blending any herb with another. Usually, you need to check the following:

- **Properties:** Understand what the herb does. *Is it calming? Stimulating? Does it aid digestion or support the immune system?*

- **Effects:** This refers to the immediate outcomes of consuming the herb. For instance, *does it make you sleepy or energized?*
- **Potential Side Effects:** Even the most beneficial herbs can have side effects, especially when consumed in large quantities or with certain other herbs or medications.

Be Cautious with Potent Herbs

While all herbs deserve respect, some demand extra attention due to their potent nature. These herbs have powerful effects even in small quantities. Combining them without proper knowledge or using them in large amounts can lead to undesirable outcomes. It is akin to adding too much spice to a dish—a little might enhance the flavor, but too much can make it inedible. Always research and perhaps even consult with an expert when dealing with potent herbs.

Interactions with Medications

Think of your body as a delicate ecosystem. Introducing something new, an herb or medication, can affect the balance. Some herbs can either boost or counteract the effects of medications. For instance, St. John's Wort, a popular herb for mood, can interfere with certain antidepressants. So, if you are taking any medications, it is not just advisable but crucial to consult with a healthcare professional before introducing new herbs to your regimen.

Start Slow

The excitement of crafting a new herbal blend can sometimes make us jump in headfirst. However, caution is key. Always begin with a smaller dose to gauge its effects. Everyone's body is different, and what works wonders for one might not sit well with another. Especially if you are making a remedy for someone else, ensure they start with a small amount. Gradually increasing the dose is easier than dealing with an adverse reaction.

Combinations to Avoid

Much like in life, not everything in herbs gets along harmoniously. While many herbs blend beautifully, offering synergistic benefits, some combinations can lead to undesirable effects or diminish the benefits of each other.

St. John's Wort and Prescription Medications

St. John's Wort, hailed for its mood-enhancing properties, is a tricky herb when it comes to combinations. It can interfere with various prescription medications, including antidepressants, birth control pills, and some heart medications. Combined, it can either intensify or weaken the effect of the medication, leading to potential health risks.

Ginger and Blood Thinners

Both ginger and blood thinners reduce the clotting ability of the blood. When combined, they can increase the risk of bleeding. Be cautious if consuming ginger in therapeutic amounts while on medications like warfarin.

Licorice Root and Hypertension Medications

While helpful in many ways, licorice root can raise blood pressure levels. When combined with hypertension medications, it can counteract the medication's effects, leading to elevated blood pressure.

Kava and Alcohol

Kava, celebrated for its calming effects, can take a dangerous turn when mixed with alcohol. Both being depressants, their combined effects can lead to severe drowsiness, impaired motor functions, and even potential liver damage.

Applications

Explore some of the primary methods through which these herbs are utilized. From drinking and ingesting to topical applications and even spiritual rituals, these age-old techniques harness the true potential of these natural remedies.

Drinking and Ingesting

The practice of drinking and ingesting herbs is about harnessing the internal benefits of the plants. Whether to alleviate a health concern or to simply enjoy the flavors, these methods have been essential in Native American wellness routines.

Infusion

Infusion involves letting a part of the plant steep in water to extract its components. This method is often likened to making tea. Placing leaves, stems, or roots in hot water and letting them sit for a while allows the water to draw out the plant's essence. For example, the leaves of the peppermint plant are frequently used in such infusions. When sipped, this brew delights the senses with its refreshing aroma, calms an upset stomach, or eases a throbbing headache.

Decoctions

While infusions are perfect for softer plant parts, certain elements like thick roots or barks require a more intensive decoction to break down and release their medicinal goodness. Slowly boiling these tougher materials in water can create a potent liquid remedy. Consider the echinacea root. Often, the roots are simmered to produce a powerful decoction. When consumed, this brew is believed to fortify the immune system, acting as a protective shield against common ailments such as colds.

Applying on Skin

The skin, the body's largest organ, often becomes the first point of contact for many ailments and discomforts. There are a lot of skin issues, from minor cuts and bruises to infections and rashes. However, the Native American herbal tradition provides a wealth of remedies tailored for topical use. By harnessing the power of these herbs, tribes have developed methods to treat, soothe, and heal various skin conditions.

Balms

Balms are semi-solid ointments crafted by blending medicinal herbs with fats, such as beeswax, lard, or olive or coconut oil. The fat or oil acts as a carrier, allowing the active compounds of the herbs to penetrate the skin more effectively. When applied, these preparations form a barrier on the skin, which not only traps moisture, aiding in hydration, but also introduces the therapeutic properties of the herbs, facilitating faster recovery.

The vibrant petals of the calendula flower are a favored choice in herbal skincare. When processed into a balm, calendula offers remarkable anti-inflammatory properties, which can combat skin redness, swelling, and even minor burns. Calendula balm is an excellent remedy for soothing irritated skin and accelerating the healing of minor wounds.

Poultices

While salves and balms are more processed, poultices offer a direct and raw way to apply herbs to the skin. Think of a poultice as a herbal plaster. Fresh or dried herbs are crushed or ground into a paste to make one. Depending on the intended effect, this paste can be mixed with water, oil, or honey. The resulting mixture is then applied directly onto the affected skin area and sometimes covered with a cloth or bandage to enhance its effectiveness.

When needing immediate action, poultices are preferable. Poultices provide quick and targeted relief in drawing out impurities from a wound, reducing sprain pain, or calming an insect bite.

Ritualistic Uses

Many Native American herbs are deeply woven into spiritual and ceremonial practices. These rituals highlight the importance of herbs in connecting with the spiritual realm and emphasize the belief in their power to harmonize and balance energies.

Smudging for Spiritual Cleansing

Smudging involves burning specific dried herbs and allowing aromatic smoke to envelop a person, place, or object. The purpose of this ritual is to cleanse negative energies and bring forth positivity and balance.

Sage, particularly in color white, is a commonly used herb for smudging. When burned, it releases a thick, aromatic smoke that purifies and sanctifies the space. This practice is often used during ceremonies, before important events, or everyday life to maintain harmony and dispel negativity.

Herbs in Ceremonies and Dances

Apart from smudging, herbs might be woven into costumes, sprinkled around ceremonial areas, or even consumed to induce specific states of consciousness. The bearberry plant, or uva ursi, is sometimes used during certain ceremonies. Its leaves are smoked in sacred pipes during specific rituals, believed to connect the participants more closely with the spiritual world.

Talismans and Protective Charms

Some people carry small pouches or bundles of specific herbs, believing they offer protection, attract positive energies, or even enhance intuition. These herbal talismans act as a bridge between the physical and spiritual realms, providing guidance and protection.

CHAPTER 3

Nutrition and Herbal Synergy

In this chapter, you will explore how food can serve as medicine and the importance of building balanced meals. Learn the unique nutritional values of native plants. Discover too how to create synergy between food and herbs through thoughtful meal planning and preparation. This chapter further highlights native superfoods that have nourished communities for generations. Finally, you will learn about crafting nourishing herbal beverages, like infusions, tonics, and elixirs.

Dietary Foundations

There is an age-old saying, *"Let food be thy medicine and medicine be thy food."* This philosophy embraces the idea that the choices you make on your food affect your overall health. Before diving into the synergy between nutrition and Native American herbs, it is essential first to grasp the fundamentals of dietary foundations. Knowing the nourishment derived from various sources makes informed decisions about your consumption.

Food as Medicine

How can your seemingly ordinary daily meals act as remedies? Civilizations from every corner of the world have held the belief that the foods you consume have the potential to heal.

When the term *'medicine'* arises in a conversation, it often conjures images of capsules, bottled syrups, or a doctor's prescription. However, envision, for a moment, a scenario where your evening meal becomes your healing potion.

Every dish you consume carries a wealth of nutrients, each serving a unique purpose. These nutrients in fruits, vegetables, grains, and proteins maintain and restore health. For instance, with deep-blue coloration, luscious blueberries have antioxidants known as anthocyanins, which neutralize harmful free radicals in the body. Such antioxidants mitigate the risks of chronic diseases, enhance memory, and even keep your skin youthful.

The Balance Act

Diet is a meticulously crafted balance of diverse nutrients to meet the body's requirements. Indigenous diets, including those of Native Americans, often integrate a harmonious mix of proteins, fats, and carbohydrates. Such a balanced intake ensures the body receives a steady energy supply, maintains optimal metabolic rates, and meets its repair and growth needs.

For instance, consuming only proteins might give your muscles the necessary amino acids, but your energy levels might dwindle without carbohydrates. Excluding healthy fats also deprives your body of essential fatty acids and fat-soluble vitamins. The magic lies in balancing nutrition.

In the high-altitude regions of South America, Native American tribes like the Incas discovered and cultivated quinoa. Labeled as the *"mother grain,"* quinoa was both sustenance and revered. Today, this grain has gained international fame. Apart from being a complete protein *(a rarity in the plant kingdom),* it is packed with fibers that promote digestive health and satiety. Moreover, it is a source of essential minerals like magnesium, manganese, and phosphorus.

Nutritional Values of Native Plants

For generations, indigenous populations have thrived by harnessing the bounty of native plants. *But what makes native plants stand out in the vast spectrum of dietary sources?*

A Wealth of Nutrients

Native plants are often *"nutrient-dense,"* which means these plants pack vitamins and minerals for relatively few calories. Yarrow, a herb historically used by Native Americans, stands out in this category. Since yarrow contains compounds that aid digestion and reduce inflammation to support wound healing.

Adapting to Harsh Conditions

Growing in diverse and sometimes unforgiving terrains, native plants have evolved to thrive under stress. This struggle often leads to accumulating phytochemicals—special compounds that protect the plant. When consumed, these compounds can confer health benefits to humans. Hence, the harsher the conditions a plant faces, the more concentrated these beneficial compounds might become.

Synergizing Food and Herbs

In culinary, herbs do not merely elevate taste but also augment nutritional value. When the timeless wisdom of Native American traditions meets modern nutrition science, a harmonious synergy between food and herbs emerges.

Meal Planning with Herbs

Incorporating herbs into meals will heighten the health benefits for the consumer.

Benefits of Using Herbs in Meals

Integrating foods with complementary herbs creates a synergy that multiplies the benefits. Understand the potential of every herb.

- **Enhancing Digestive Harmony:** Some meals might sit heavy in your stomach. But thoughtfully incorporating herbs known for digestive properties, like mint or fennel, ensures a smoother digestive process. Meals you eat are then broken down more effectively, leading to a more relaxed post-meal experience.
- **Boosting Nutrient Bioavailability:** Some foods are nutrient-dense, but the body's ability to absorb these nutrients can sometimes be limited. Adding herbs helps your body get the most out of your foods. For instance, a black pepper facilitates better absorption of the beneficial compounds in turmeric.

- **Fortifying Antioxidant Defense:** The body is constantly exposed to external stressors. Combining antioxidant-rich foods with herbs packed with these protective compounds builds a line of defense. It is like doubling up on shields, ensuring that cells are better equipped to fend off potential threats.

The Art of Pairing

Marrying various herbs and ingredients can produce a harmonious taste. Turmeric, with its golden hue and anti-inflammatory properties, becomes even more potent when paired with black pepper. The piperine in black pepper enhances the absorption of curcumin, turmeric's primary compound.

To help you get started, here are some tips:

- **Understand the Herb:** Take the time to learn about the taste, aroma, and health benefits of each herb. Knowing what an herb brings to the table ensures it is used most effectively.
- **Complementary Pairing:** Combine herbs and foods that not only taste great together but also mutually reinforce their health benefits.
- **Experiment and Explore:** Culinary art thrives on creativity. Seek new ideas. You might find that unconventional herb and food pairings result in the most delightful and nutritious dishes.

Native Superfoods

Before superfoods started trending in health blogs, indigenous communities had already identified and utilized the nutrition-packed powerhouses. These native superfoods, often staples in their diets, held the secrets to vitality and well-being.

From the lush forests to the vast plains, Native American diets were a diverse collection of powerful, nutrient-rich foods. Blueberries, for instance, defend the body against harmful free radicals. Meanwhile, chia seeds, with their rich omega-3 content, were an energy source, ensuring stamina for daily activities.

Some examples of native superfoods include the following:

- **Quinoa:** Originally cultivated by Andean cultures, this grain-like seed is packed with protein, fiber, and essential nutrients, including magnesium, phosphorus, and manganese.
- **Echinacea:** Native to North America, echinacea was traditionally used by Native American tribes to treat various ailments, from colds to wounds. Today, it is widely recognized for its immune-boosting properties.
- **Sage:** Native Americans have used sage for its antimicrobial and antiseptic properties. The herb is commonly used in smudging ceremonies but also has culinary uses and is rich in antioxidants.
- **Wild Bergamot (Monarda):** Not to be confused with the bergamot orange, this North American native plant was used by Native Americans as a medicinal herb. The leaves were often made into tea to treat respiratory issues. The plant is also rich in antioxidants.

- **Pawpaw:** Though it is a fruit-bearing tree rather than an herb, pawpaw has medicinal leaves and bark used traditionally by Native Americans for various remedies. The fruit itself is a rich source of vitamins and minerals.

Herbal Dishes Ideas

Some herbal dishes to try on are listed as follows:

Savory Sage Soup

Sage, with silvery-green leaves, has been a prized herb for centuries. With its distinctive aroma, sage is a repository of antioxidants that can combat oxidative stress in the body.

Ingredients

- 2 cups of diced potatoes or butternut squash
- 1 onion, chopped
- 2 garlic cloves, minced
- 2 tablespoons of fresh sage, chopped
- 4 cups of vegetable broth
- Salt and pepper to taste
- Cream or coconut milk for a touch of richness *(optional)*

Instructions

1. In a pot, sauté onions and garlic until translucent.
2. Add potatoes or squash, sage, and vegetable broth.
3. Simmer until the vegetables are tender.
4. Blend the mixture until smooth. Stir in cream or coconut milk if desired. Season with salt and pepper.
5. Serve hot, garnished with a sprinkle of chopped sage.

Minty Quinoa Salad

Apart from its refreshing taste, mint is known to soothe the digestive system.

Ingredients

- 2 cups cooked quinoa
- 1 cup roasted vegetables *(like bell peppers, zucchini, and carrots)*
- 1/4 cup freshly chopped mint
- 3 tablespoons of olive oil
- Juice of 1 lemon
- Salt and pepper to taste

Instructions

1. In a large bowl, mix quinoa, roasted vegetables, and mint.
2. Whisk together olive oil, lemon juice, salt, and pepper in a separate bowl to make the vinaigrette.
3. Drizzle the vinaigrette over the quinoa mixture and toss well.
4. Serve chilled or at room temperature.

Rosemary Roasted Vegetables

Rosemary imparts a woody aroma to dishes. Moreover, it is believed to have anti-inflammatory effects and can enhance cognitive functions.

Ingredients

- 4 cups of mixed vegetables *(potatoes, carrots, bell peppers, etc.)*
- 2 tablespoons of olive oil
- 2 tablespoons of fresh rosemary, chopped
- Salt and pepper to taste

Instructions

1. Preheat the oven to 400 °F (200 °C).
2. Toss vegetables with olive oil, rosemary, salt, and pepper in a large bowl.
3. Spread them evenly on a baking sheet.
4. Roast for 25 to 30 minutes or until vegetables are tender and slightly caramelized.
5. Serve hot as a side dish.

Sage and Wild Bergamot-Infused Grilled Chicken

Sage, known for its antiseptic and antimicrobial qualities, gives the chicken an earthy note. Wild bergamot brings a hint of citrusy and minty tones to the dish.

Ingredients

- 4 chicken breasts
- 2 tablespoons of olive oil
- 1 tablespoon of fresh sage, chopped
- 1 tablespoon of fresh wild bergamot leaves, chopped *(or dried, if fresh is not available)*
- Zest and juice of 1 lemon
- Salt and pepper to taste

Instructions

1. Mix olive oil, sage, wild bergamot, lemon zest, lemon juice, salt, and pepper in a bowl.
2. Marinate the chicken breasts in this mixture for at least 2 hours.
3. Grill the chicken over medium heat until fully cooked, frequently basting with the leftover marinade.
4. Serve hot with your choice of side.

Herbal Beverages

Did you know many herbal concoctions are rooted in ancient traditions, especially in Native American cultures? Learn more about these herbal beverages.

Infusions

For those new to the world of herbal beverages, infusions are an easy starting point. The essence of an infusion lies in immersing herbs in hot water and letting time do the rest. The versatility of infusions allows you to mix and match, creating combinations that cater to your palate and well-being.

Examples:

- **Echinacea Infusion:** Help fight off colds and other infections. It offers a slightly tingling sensation and a complex flavor profile, making it a comforting choice during flu season.

- **Sage Infusion:** A sage infusion serves multiple purposes, from serving as a natural antimicrobial to aiding in digestion. Simply steep the leaves in hot water.
- **Dandelion Infusion:** Often regarded as a mere weed, dandelions are nutritional powerhouses. An infusion made from its leaves or roots aids in digestion and serves as a mild diuretic.

Native American Tonics

Tonics, infused with the knowledge of generations past, hold a special place in the herbal traditions of the indigenous peoples of America. Such beverages aim to strengthen and invigorate the body. Unlike momentary remedies, tonics are designed for regular consumption, helping to maintain or restore vitality and health over time.

Examples:

- **Wormwood Tonic:** A herb native to temperate regions but has been used in various traditional medicine systems, including Native American herbal practices. Some tribes have utilized wormwood for its potential to aid in digestion, relieve indigestion, and even treat intestinal worms. A tonic made from wormwood can offer a bitter, aromatic experience stimulating the digestive system.
- **Devil's Claw Tonic:** A plant native to Africa but has found a place in various indigenous pharmacopeias, including some Native American practices, after its introduction to the Americas. Devil's claw is used for its anti-inflammatory properties and is believed to offer relief from various

pains, such as back pain and arthritis. A tonic made from devil's claw can provide a natural option for managing inflammation and pain.

Elixirs

Derived from the Arabic word *"al-Iksir,"* which means *"miracle substances,"* elixirs have long been associated with healing and longevity. These concentrated liquid solutions contain one or more active ingredients dissolved in alcohol or another solvent. Often enriched with additional components like honey, lemon, or various spices, elixirs meld flavor with function. Unlike tonics, which focus on revitalizing and strengthening, elixirs aim at curative and preventive wellness.

Examples:

- **Fernleaf Biscuit Root Elixir:** Fernleaf Biscuit Root, also known as Lomatium dissectum, has been traditionally used by Native American tribes for its antiviral and antibacterial properties. It was often employed for treating respiratory issues and infections. An elixir from its roots can be used as an immune system booster and a natural remedy for colds and flu.
- **Wild Bergamot Elixir:** Wild Bergamot, or Monarda fistulosa, is native to North America and was traditionally used by Native Americans to treat respiratory issues and infections. An elixir from steeping the leaves or flowers in hot water can be calming and uplifting, offering a unique combination of mint and citrus flavors. The antiseptic properties of the plant also make it beneficial for oral health.

Exercise: Crafting Your Herbal Dish

To understand and experience the synergy between nutrition and herbs by creating a personalized dish. Through hands-on engagement, participants will learn about integrating native plant-based ingredients and herbs into daily meals. This exercise also aims to foster a deeper appreciation for the combined benefits and flavors that herbs bring to nutrition.

Materials:

- A choice of native plant-based ingredients *(e.g., vegetables, fruits, nuts, seeds, grains)*
- 1-2 herbs of your choice *(e.g., basil, rosemary, mint, dill, etc.)*
- Basic kitchen utensils *(bowl, knife, cutting board)*
- Olive oil, salt, pepper *(optional)*

Instructions:

1. **Research and Reflect**: Spend 10 minutes reading about the nutritional values of your chosen native plant-based ingredients. Take note of one or two health benefits of each. Research the herbs you have selected. *What are their health benefits? How do they synergize with your chosen ingredients?*
2. **Brainstorm a Dish.** Based on your research, brainstorm a simple dish incorporating your chosen ingredients and herbs. It could be as simple as a salad, a grain bowl, a smoothie, or a stir-fry. Consider how the flavor and benefits of the herbs complement the other ingredients.
3. **Preparation**: Wash and prep your ingredients.
   - *Salad:* Chop ingredients and mix them in a bowl. Add a simple dressing, perhaps olive oil, with a squeeze of lemon, salt, and pepper. Toss in your herbs.

- ○ *Smoothie:* Blend your ingredients with water or a milk alternative. Add your herbs and blend until smooth.
- ○ For other dishes, combine ingredients that make sense to you, ensuring the herbs are integrated well.
4. **Enjoy and Reflect**: Savor your dish mindfully. As you eat, think about the synergy of the herbs and ingredients. *Can you taste the herbs? Do they enhance the overall flavor of the dish? Reflect on how you feel after eating. Energized? Satisfied?*
5. **Journal**: Take a few minutes to jot down your dish, the ingredients and herbs used, and any observations about taste, synergy, and how you felt after consuming it.

CHAPTER 4

Safety, Ethics, and Conservation

As you go deeper into the world of Native American herbs and their many applications, it is imperative to approach this journey with a lens of caution and conscientiousness. While the medicinal and nutritional virtues of these plants have been time-tested through centuries of indigenous wisdom, do note that not all herbs are suitable for everyone. Just as modern pharmaceuticals come with guidelines for proper use, so too do these natural remedies require a responsible approach.

This chapter guides responsibly approaching herbalism. It discusses identifying and avoiding toxic plants, establishing proper dosages, and monitoring for adverse reactions. You will also learn optimal timing for harvesting herbs and employing sustainable collection techniques that respect plant life cycles. Additionally, it explores the deeper spiritual relationship many indigenous cultures have with plant spirits. Finally, the chapter examines conservation efforts and the importance of preserving threatened medicinal plants for future generations. With this knowledge, you can begin utilizing herbal wisdom safely and sustainably.

Safeguarding Health

Despite being helpful, some herbs are toxic when consumed. To safeguard your health, learn to safe plants from potentially toxic ones.

Importance of Proper Identification

The ability to recognize toxic plants is particularly crucial for a few reasons, even if your primary source of herbs is from trusted suppliers:

Foraging and Wildcrafting

Although most people will purchase herbs from reputable sources, foraging or wildcrafting—*gathering herbs from their natural, wild habitat*—is experiencing a resurgence. In such instances, distinguishing between toxic and non-toxic plants is a matter of utmost importance. Many beneficial plants have toxic look-alikes. For example, echinacea has a poisonous doppelgänger known as the purple coneflower *(Echinacea angustifolia),* which can cause various health issues if ingested.

Commercial Vendors

Even when purchasing from commercial vendors, knowing what the authentic plant looks like can help judge the quality of the herbs you buy. Inferior or incorrectly harvested plants may inadvertently mix with toxic variants, posing potential risks. Your ability to recognize plants can be an extra layer of quality control.

Home Gardening

Some enthusiastic individuals may cultivate their herbs in a small indoor pot or a full-fledged garden. Accidental ingestion of a toxic plant—*either by mistaking it for something else or due to cross-contamination in the garden*—can happen. Understanding the visual identifiers of toxic plants is a safety net.

Tips for Identifying Toxic Plants

For you to develop this skill, follow these tips:

- **Research Before Use:** Knowledge is the first line of defense against toxic plants. Before introducing any herb into your diet, extensively research it. Books specifically on Native American herbs or reputable online databases can be invaluable in this process. Also, look for scientific names, as common names vary across regions and might lead to confusion.
- **Consult Experts:** When in doubt, turn to the experts. Herbalists, botanists, or those specializing in Native American plants can provide guidance.
- **Invest in Field Guides:** For those who frequently explore the outdoors or have a penchant for foraging, investing in a good field guide can be a game-changer. These guides, often with pictures and descriptions, help you identify plants accurately.
- **Join Workshops or Groups:** Many communities offer workshops on plant identification and herbal preparations. Joining such sessions can provide hands-on experience and knowledge sharing.

- **Avoid Wild Harvesting Without Knowledge:** The wilderness is full of look-alikes. Refrain from wild harvesting until you are confident in your ability to distinguish between the two.
- **Taste Test (with Caution!):** If you believe a plant is safe but are unsure, perform a taste test. First, touch the plant to your lips, then the tip of your tongue. Wait a few minutes to ensure no burning, itching, or numbness. If it is safe, chew a bit, but do not swallow immediately. Perform this method with extreme caution and preferably under the guidance of someone experienced.
- **Photograph Unknown Plants:** As you come across an unfamiliar plant, take clear photographs of it—focusing on leaves, stems, flowers, and roots. These pictures can later be shared with experts or compared with online resources for identification.

Safe Dosages and Intake

Taking herbal beverages demands a deep understanding of dosages for a dual purpose: *ensuring the safety of the consumer and achieving the desired health benefits.* Overindulging in herbal beverages leads to unexpected or harmful reactions, while consuming too little may offer no perceptible benefit.

Potency

Each herb carries its distinct potency—a measure of its strength and effect on your body. This variation makes one herbal beverage vastly different from another in terms of impact. To illustrate, while a soothing cup of chamomile tea might be perfect for unwinding after a long day, multiple cups of valerian root tea could push you into a deep sedative state, potentially leading to drowsiness.

Guidelines for Safe Intake

The guidelines outlined below will help you navigate herbal consumption, ensuring that you harness the plants' potent properties without jeopardizing your well-being.

1. **Start Small:** Especially when trying a new herbal beverage, it is essential to introduce it to your system gradually. Doing so will allow you to gauge its effects and ensure no immediate adverse reactions occur. For teas, begin with a weaker brew by using less of the herb or steeping for a shorter time. Gradually increase the strength as you become accustomed to its effects.

2. **Follow Recommendations:** Every herbal beverage has guidelines, often rooted in ancient traditions or modern research. Adhering to these ensures that you reap the benefits without courting danger. Refer to reputable sources, such as books on Native American herbs, or consult with herbalists. They can provide specific brewing times quantities and even suggest complementary herbs for a synergistic effect.

3. **Listen to Your Body:** Your body, with its unique constitution and sensitivities, is the best indicator of how an herb affects you. Pay close attention to subtle and pronounced changes after consuming an herbal beverage. *Are you feeling too relaxed, jittery, or perhaps nauseous?* These could signal that you must adjust the dosage or discontinue that herb.

4. **Maintain a Consumption Log:** Keeping track of what you consume and what amounts can provide invaluable insights over time. Note down the name of the herb, the quantity, brewing time, and any effects *(positive or negative)* you observed.

5. **Seek Personalized Guidance:** General recommendations are a great starting point, but personal guidance tailored to your health conditions, preferences, and body constitution can be even more beneficial. Consider scheduling a session with a herbalist or a naturopathic doctor. These professionals can offer advice, suggest alternatives, or tweak recommendations to fit your needs.

Monitoring Reactions and Allergies

Allergies and adverse reactions can sneak up unexpectedly as you consume certain herbs. Knowing how to spot early signs of allergies and take appropriate measures is necessary.

- **Itching or Rashes:** The first sign of an allergic skin reaction. Redness, itchiness, or small bumps could indicate your body's resistance to a particular herb.
- **Shortness of Breath or Wheezing:** Any difficulty in breathing or a wheezing sound when you breathe should be addressed immediately.
- **Swelling of the Face, Lips, or Tongue:** Any unexpected swelling around the facial area can indicate a severe allergic reaction known as angioedema.
- **Nausea or Stomach Upset:** While some herbs can naturally cause a mild stomach upset due to their properties, persistent nausea or intense stomach pain can indicate an adverse reaction.

Precautionary Steps

The following are precautionary guidelines to avoid consuming herbs that could trigger allergic reactions.

1. **Patch Test:** Before sipping a full cup of a new herbal beverage, check for any topical allergic reactions. To do this, brew a small amount of the herbal beverage. Once cooled, apply a few drops to the inner side of your wrist or elbow. Cover with a bandage and wait for 24 hours. If there is no redness or itching, you can consume the beverage, starting with a smaller quantity.

2. **Stay Informed:** Familiarizing yourself with common allergens can help avoid potential pitfalls. Regularly update yourself with information on herbs, especially those known to cause allergies. Websites, journals, or books on herbal studies can be invaluable resources.

3. **Maintain a Reaction Diary:** Tracking your experiences with different herbs can help identify patterns or specific herbs that do not sit well with your system. Make a note of each herb you consume, the quantity, date, and any reactions, no matter how mild. Over time, this can offer insights into which herbs to approach with caution or avoid entirely.

4. **Seek Medical Attention:** Some reactions, especially severe ones, require immediate medical intervention. If you experience intense reactions like difficulty breathing, chest pain, prolonged dizziness, or fainting, contact emergency services or head to the nearest medical facility. Always inform the medical professional about the herb you consumed.

5. **Consult Before Consumption:** If you have a history of allergies or are on medications, it is always safer to consult before introducing a new herb. Speak with a healthcare provider with knowledge of herbal remedies about potential interactions or allergic reactions.

Ethical Harvesting

As enthusiasts, consumers, or cultivators of Native American herbs, you are responsible for ensuring that your engagement with nature remains sustainable, respectful, and beneficial for all involved. Ethical harvesting is a principle that ensures the gifts of nature remain abundant for generations to come.

Right Times to Harvest

Just as the quality of fruits and vegetables is affected when picked, the potency of herbs is closely tied to their harvesting time. In other words, each herb has its *"prime time"* for harvest, a peak moment for its medicinal properties. Tuning into these natural cycles maximizes the efficacy of your herbal remedies while also being a responsible steward of the plant's continued well-being.

Seasonal Awareness

The constituents or active compounds in a plant can vary throughout the year. Harvesting during the plant's peak ensures the maximum concentration of these compounds.

- **Spring:** The season of rebirth. Many herbs sprout fresh, young leaves during spring. These leaves, tender and filled with the energy of the new season, are often packed with nutrients. Examples include dandelion greens and nettles.

- **Summer:** As the sun warms the Earth, flowers bloom, and seeds mature. Late summer is especially essential for harvesting herbs like wild bergamot or bee balm, whose flowers are in full, radiant bloom.
- **Fall:** Roots become the focal point in fall. As the plant prepares for winter, energy is stored in the roots. Herbs like burdock and, as previously mentioned, ginseng, have roots rich in medicinal properties during this time.
- **Winter:** Though seemingly dormant, some hardy herbs can still be harvested in winter. Evergreens like white pine can be collected, their needles made into a refreshing tea filled with Vitamin C.

Plant Lifecycle

Plants are categorized into three main types based on their lifecycles:

- **Annuals:** These are plants that sprout, grow, flower, seed, and die all within a single year. Harvesting them at the right time, generally, before they seed, maximizes their beneficial properties. Sweet basil is an example of an annual herb.
- **Biennials:** These plants have a two-year lifecycle. In the first year, such plants focus on vegetative growth, typically producing leaves. In the second year, they flower, seed, and eventually die. Knowing which year of the lifecycle you are in helps you decide whether to harvest leaves, seeds, or roots. Mullein is a well-known biennial herb.
- **Perennials:** Unlike annuals and biennials, perennials come back year after year. These plants may offer different parts for harvesting at various stages of their lifecycle. For instance, Goldenseal, a valuable herb in Native American tradition, is a perennial often harvested for its

roots. However, employ sustainable harvesting methods to ensure the plant's longevity.

Sustainable Collection Techniques

Ethical harvesting techniques ensure not only the longevity of herbs but also the preservation of indigenous traditions tied to them.

Percentage Rule

Sustainability begins with restraint. Ensure that plant populations regenerate and flourish after harvesting. Overharvesting diminishes plant populations, making them vulnerable to extinction. With certain herbs having cultural and medicinal roles in Native American communities, their depletion could be a tremendous loss. Always survey the area and estimate the number of plants present. Harvest only a small fraction, allowing the majority to mature, seed, and replenish.

Tools Matter

Dull or dirty tools cause unnecessary harm, making plants susceptible to diseases or hindering their ability to recover. Regularly sharpen and clean your tools. Scissors, pruners, or knives should be sterilized, especially if moving between different harvesting sites, to prevent the spread of plant diseases.

Whole-Plant Harvesting

Deciding to harvest a plant, including its roots, should be made with great care. Roots are the life anchors of plants, and harvesting them ends the plant's life cycle. The decision also depends on the type of herb you are dealing with—some herbs are specifically cultivated for their roots. These should be chosen with full aware-ness of their population status and ecological role.

Goldenseal is often harvested for its roots due to its medicinal properties. When harvesting Goldenseal, only collect from abun-dant populations and be certain to have the necessary permis-sions, especially if you are on protected or indigenous lands. After harvesting, it is considered good practice to sow Goldenseal seeds in the area to encourage regrowth and sustainability.

Being a Conscientious Harvester

Every herb you responsibly harvest ensures that future genera-tions experience the wonder and healing these plants offer. Your role is not just that of a gatherer but a guardian of age-old tradi-tions and natural treasures.

Respecting Plant Spirits

Harvesting plants is a sacred interaction with a sentient being to these indigenous communities. This reverence towards plant spir-its is fundamental to Native American herbal practices. Stay re-spectful to plant spirits by doing the following:

Seek Permission

The act of asking for permission is rooted deeply in Native Amer-ican traditions, emphasizing a harmonious relationship with na-ture. Plants, to indigenous people, are akin to sentient beings. Asking permission acknowledges the plant's spirit and life force. It emphasizes the harvester's understanding of taking something valuable and the hope for mutual respect. Before harvesting, take a moment of stillness. Communicate your intentions to the plant, verbally or mentally, showing reverence for its life and gifts.

Offerings

Leaving an offering is a symbolic act of gratitude, ensuring the cycle of giving and taking remains balanced. Offerings convey appreciation and are believed to appease plant spirits. They represent a cycle of reciprocity, a way to give back to what has been taken. Traditional offerings include items like tobacco, a potent symbol in Native American culture. Any genuine token or gesture of gratitude, from water to organic compost, can serve as an offering.

Intention Matters

Harvesting with intention ensures that the act is done mindfully and respectfully. When harvested with good intentions, plants are believed to offer maximum therapeutic benefits. It strengthens the bond between the harvester and the plant, ensuring the utmost respect is given. Before harvesting, understand the purpose of your collection. *Are you gathering for medicinal purposes, spiritual rituals, or culinary use?* Keeping this intention in mind ensures you only take what is needed and respectfully approach the task.

Conservation Efforts

Over time, several medicinal plants have become threatened due to various human activities, making their conservation vital. Expanding urban areas, aggressive agricultural practices, and climate change, among other factors, have put numerous medicinal plants at risk. Overharvesting, particularly without sustainable practices, further exacerbates the situation.

Examples include:

- Goldenseal
- American Ginseng
- Osha Root
- Black Cohosh

Losing these plants would mean losing an integral part of history and traditional knowledge.

Native Community Initiatives

Many indigenous communities have taken the mantle to protect and preserve herbal legacies.

- **Seed Bank:** Several Native American tribes have initiated seed banks, ensuring the preservation of native plant species. These banks serve as repositories, safeguarding seeds for future generations.
- **Educational Programs:** Through community-driven programs, young generations are educated about the importance of medicinal plants, sustainable harvesting techniques, and the cultural significance of these herbs.
- **Restoration Projects:** Indigenous communities often undertake reforestation and habitat restoration endeavors. Planting native species in their traditional habitats ensures their survival and proliferation.

Partnering for Preservation

Various partnerships have been established between indigenous communities, conservationists, and governmental agencies.

- **Collaborative Research:** By combining traditional indigenous knowledge with modern botanical science, efforts are being made to understand better and address the threats these plants face.
- **Financial Grants:** Government and private entities provide funds to support conservation projects. These funds aid in research, habitat restoration, and the development of sustainable harvesting techniques.
- **Shared Responsibilities:** It is not just the responsibility of Native American communities. Conservation is a global concern, and the impact is magnified when multiple stakeholders come together. For instance, the United Plant Savers, an organization dedicated to conserving native medicinal plants, often collaborates with indigenous tribes to enhance preservation efforts.

Exercise: Ethical Harvesting Scavenger Hunt

Learn how to immerse yourself in nature while learning the principles of ethical harvesting through this exercise.

Materials Needed:

- A notebook or small piece of paper.
- A pen or pencil.
- A timer or stopwatch *(optional)*.

Instructions:

1. **Setting Up:** Go to your backyard, a local park, or any natural place to find plants. Then, set a timer for 20 minutes *(optional, but it adds a fun challenge).*

2. **The Hunt:** Here are some ideas of plats you can look for:
   - ◦ ***Find a Plant Past its Prime:*** Search for a plant that has already completed its lifecycle, such as a dried-up flower or brown leaf.
   - ◦ ***Spot a Crowded Area:*** Identify a location where plants are densely packed.
   - ◦ ***Discover a Young Plant:*** Find a seedling or a very young plant.
   - ◦ ***Leave No Trace:*** Move carefully to avoid trampling on plants or disrupting habitats.

3. **Jot Down Observations:** For each of the above, note down in your notebook:
   - ◦ Name or description of the plant.
   - ◦ Reason for choosing it for that category.
   - ◦ One action you can take to harvest or support the plant's growth and survival ethically.

4. **Reflection & Share:** After the hunt, reflect on the activity. *Did it make you more aware of ethical harvesting principles?* You can also share your findings with a friend or family member and explain the ethical harvesting principles behind your scavenger hunt.

Notes:

While engaging with the environment, keep these guiding notes at the forefront of your exploration:

- **Find a Plant Past its Prime:** Search for a plant that has already completed its lifecycle, such as a dried-up flower or a brown leaf. Such a step embodies the principle of harvesting at the right time, emphasizing the importance of recognizing when a plant has reached the end of its lifecycle.

- **Spot a Crowded Area:** Identify where plants are densely packed together. This scenario underlines the importance of sustainable collection, showcasing that taking one plant might not harm the ecosystem due to its abundance in such environments.

- **Discover a Young Plant:** Spot a seedling or a very young plant. It will serve as a reminder of the principle of allowing plants to grow, mature, and reproduce before considering them for harvesting, highlighting the importance of patience and foresight.

- **Leave No Trace:** As you navigate through your environment, tread lightly. Ensure you do not trample on plants or disrupt habitats, embodying the ethos of minimizing human impact and respecting the sanctity of natural spaces.

CHAPTER 5

Designing a Healing Garden

Gardening can be a rewarding and therapeutic activity that allows you to connect with nature. If you want to cultivate a healing garden filled with Native American medicinal herbs, this chapter will guide you through the fundamentals. You will learn how to choose the right herbs for your needs, understand their ideal soil and sunlight requirements, and properly care for the plants. The chapter also provides tips on natural pest control methods to protect your garden and best practices for gentle harvesting and proper storage once your herbs are ready.

Garden Basics

When it comes to growing a healing garden, specifically filled with Native American herbs, there are a few basics that every enthusiast should be familiar with, such as:

Choosing Herbs

As you prepare to design a healing garden brimming with Native American herbs, selecting your plants becomes essential. These herbs, steeped in rich history and profound benefits, can transform your garden into a reservoir of wellness and spirituality. By considering your goals, understanding each herb's natural requirements, and ensuring appropriate spacing, you can curate a garden that resonates with purpose.

Note the following:

- **Know Your Purpose.** Begin by clarifying your intentions.
  - **Medicinal Uses:** If your primary goal is to cultivate a medicine cabinet in your backyard, there are numerous herbs to consider. Beyond echinacea, which bolsters the immune system, herbs like yarrow can help with minor wounds, and black cohosh can alleviate certain symptoms of menopause.
  - **Culinary Delights:** Many Native American herbs not only have medicinal properties but are also culinary treasures. While sage adds flavor to dishes, herbs like wild bergamot (often called bee balm) can create aromatic teas.
  - **Spiritual and Ritualistic Practices:** Some herbs, like white sage and sweetgrass, are deeply rooted in Native American spiritual practices used for purification and bringing positivity.
- **Research the Herb's Native Conditions:** Every herb has its sweet spot, a set of conditions where it naturally flourishes. Before you begin planting or harvesting,

research what those conditions are. Some of these are the following:

- ○ **Climate Compatibility:** Opt for herbs naturally at home in cooler climates in an area with chilly winters. For instance, goldenseal is a woodland native well-suited for less balmy environments, unlike herbs that thrive in desert conditions.

- ○ **Sunlight Requirements:** Just like some people are sun-worshippers while others prefer the shade, herbs have sunlight preferences. Sunflowers, for example, cannot get enough sun, while woodland tobacco is happier in the softer, filtered light you would find under a forest canopy. Place your herbs in spots that match their love or dislike of direct sunlight.

- ○ **Soil Preferences:** Herbs are as choosy about their soil as some people are about their vacation spots. For example, sand cherry is quite happy in sandy soil, while wild ginger prefers the rich, damp soil you typically find in a forest. Knowing what type of soil your chosen herbs prefer can determine how well they grow.

- • **Space and Size Consideration:** Giving your herbs room to breathe and grow is fundamental.

- ○ **Height and Spread:** Visualize your garden's future, considering the full-grown size of your chosen herbs. For example, echinacea plants might reach 4 feet, while ramps (wild leeks) might prefer to stay low. Be mindful of the space each plant will need as it matures.

- ○ **Companion Planting:** Some Native American herbs naturally support each other's growth. Pairing bearberry with juniper, for instance, creates a symbiotic relationship as both plants thrive in similar soil conditions. Find out which Native American herbs are compatible in terms of soil, water, and sunlight needs.

Soil Needs

Soil and water are the lifeblood of your garden, playing an integral role in ensuring your herbs grow lush and healthy. Understanding these elements is like knowing the ABCs of gardening.

Soil Types

Think of soil as a recipe with various ingredients. Like how different dishes call for specific ingredients, certain herbs thrive best in particular soil types.

- **Clay Soil:** Dense and sticky when wet, clay soil has excellent water storage but may lack proper drainage. Plants that can handle such conditions include purple coneflower and wild strawberry.
- **Sandy Soil:** As you rightly pointed out, sandy soil is all about drainage. While great for drought-tolerant herbs like yucca, it might need frequent watering due to its rapid moisture loss.
- **Silt Soil:** Silty soil feels smooth and holds moisture longer than sandy soil. It is fertile and good for most plants but can compact easily. Herbs like wild onions thrive here.

- **Loamy Soil:** Often deemed the gold standard for gardeners, loamy soil is a balanced blend of sand, silt, and clay. It combines the best of all soil types, providing moisture while ensuring adequate drainage. A broad range of herbs, from mint to chamomile, cherish this type.

Enriching Your Soil

Regardless of type, remember that soil health can be enhanced. Composting, for example, can improve nutrient content and texture, benefiting your herbs immensely. In making your soil healthy, do as follows:

- **Maintain pH Balance:** Just like humans have a preferred body temperature, plants have a favored soil pH, which absorbs nutrients best. Beyond testing kits, some natural signs can hint at soil acidity or alkalinity. For example, if you notice ferns and moss, your soil might be acidic. As you mentioned, lime can raise soil pH, making it more alkaline. Conversely, if you want to acidify your soil, organic matter like pine needles or coffee grounds can be of assistance.
- **Incorporate Micro-nutrients:** Micro-nutrients like iron, manganese, and zinc aid photosynthesis and disease resistance.
- **Water Wisely:** Too much or too little watering can spell disaster. Drip irrigation systems can provide a steady supply of water, reducing waste. If watering by hand, aim close to the roots, minimizing moisture loss through evaporation.

- **Understand Your Herb's Origins:** A herb native to the desert will have different water needs than one from a rainforest. Studying their natural habitats can give clues about their watering preferences.
- **Try Mulching.** Mulch, straw, wood chips, or leaves can regulate soil temperature and reduce evaporation, ensuring consistent moisture levels.

Keeping Plants Healthy

Tending to your plants' needs, ensuring they are free from diseases, and protecting them from pests are like the parental care given to children. Taking proactive steps and embracing natural solutions can guarantee the survival of your precious herbs. Follow the guide below to keep plants healthy.

Regular Inspection

Regular observation can unveil problems before they balloon into major concerns. When inspecting, check for these:

- **Growth Patterns:** If a plant that usually grows upright begins to sprawl, it might be seeking more light. Conversely, browning leaf tips might indicate excessive sunlight.
- **Root Health:** Occasionally, it is worth inspecting the roots, especially if the plant appears unhealthy. Soft, brown roots can be a sign of overwatering, while hard, shriveled roots might mean the plant is thirsty.
- **Undersides of Leaves:** Many pests prefer the leaf's underside, like aphids. A regular flip-check can spot these tiny invaders early on.

Pruning and Deadheading

Removing dead or diseased parts of the plant directs the plant's energy towards healthy growth. In densely growing herbs like rosemary, thinning can improve air circulation, reducing the risk of fungal diseases. Additionally, removing spent flowers from herbs like calendula encourages continuous blooming. Doing so not only prolongs the beauty of your garden but also promotes the overall well-being of your herbal plants.

Advanced Care for Your Healing Garden

Explore the advanced techniques of companion planting and natural pest control. These methods ensure not just the growth but also the holistic well-being of your garden. Embrace these practices, and watch as your healing garden thrives, becoming both a sanctuary for plants and a testament to your evolving green thumb.

Companion Planting

Harnessing the power of companion planting is like creating harmonious friendships in your garden, where each plant brings out the best in the other. Many Native American herbs can benefit from companions, some of which are:

- **Sage and Lavender:** Sage, often used for its purifying qualities, pairs well with lavender. While sage deters pests like cabbage moths, lavender attracts pollinators.
- **Yarrow and Basil:** Yarrow, known for its healing properties, can enhance the aroma and flavor of basil. In return, basil can deter pests from the yarrow.

Natural Pest Control

Chemical pesticides often have a broad spectrum of action that can also kill beneficial insects, disrupting natural ecosystems. Such chemicals also leach into the soil and waterways, causing further harm to wildlife and, in some cases, humans. Some ways to manage pests naturally without using chemical pesticides include the following:

Beneficial Insects

Not all insects are adversaries in your garden. Several play roles in checking the populations of harmful pests, such as:

- **Ladybugs:** Tiny, spotted soldiers, voracious predators of aphids, scale insects, and mites. By creating an environment conducive to ladybugs, such as planting dill or yarrow, you will have a dedicated troop guarding your herbs.
- **Praying Mantises:** These insect's camouflage allows them to ambush unsuspecting pests, including beetles, caterpillars, and other harmful insects. Encouraging a mantis population means having an active patrol against larger pests.
- **Spiders:** Incredible pest controllers, trapping flies, mosquitoes, and other pests in their intricate webs.

Plants as Protectors

Beyond plants' healing properties, some possess inherent mechanisms to repel pests, making them natural sentinels for your garden.

- **Chrysanthemums:** The pyrethrin chrysanthemums produce naturally repels bugs. Planted around your garden to have a defensive ring against pests like aphids and spider mites.
- **Lemongrass:** Its lemony aroma is a deterrent for pests, especially mosquitoes. Planting lemongrass can create a fragrant barrier, ensuring your healing garden remains a no-fly zone for these pesky insects.
- **Garlic and Onions:** Repel many pests due to their strong scent. Interspersing them in your garden can deter pests like slugs and carrot flies.

Barriers and Traps:

Sometimes, the old ways are the best. Before the advent of commercial pesticides, physical barriers were often used to protect plants, such as:

- **Row Covers:** Think of these as protective blankets for your plants. Lightweight and absorbent, it allows sunlight and water to pass through, preventing moths, beetles, and other pests from reaching your plants.
- **Neem Oil:** A potent deterrent for a variety of pests. When sprayed, it forms a protective layer, keeping pests at bay without affecting beneficial insects like bees.
- **Diatomaceous Earth:** A naturally occurring sedimentary rock, it can be sprinkled around plants. Its microscopic sharp edges deter pests like slugs and beetles, making them think twice before approaching.

Proper Harvesting

Proper harvesting ensures that the benefits you derive from your herbs are optimized, preserving their medicinal, aromatic, and culinary attributes.

Determine the Right Time

The health and quality of an herb are closely tied to its life cycle, and harvesting at the right moment ensures you capture the plant's benefits at their zenith.

- **Morning Harvest:** Harvesting in the early morning, after the dew has settled but before the sun is high and intense, ensures that the plant's oils are most concentrated. Doing so ensures the herbs are still refreshed from the night, not yet bearing the full brunt of the day's heat.
- **Flowering Phase:** Herbs often reach their pinnacle of potency right on the cusp of their flowering phase. The plant channels its energy into producing essential oils and other compounds just before blooming. For instance, when tending herbs like thyme or rosemary, harvest them when the buds are evident but not fully opened.

Gentle Handling

Herbs are delicate. Any roughness can compromise their quality. Follow the tips below when handling your plants.

- **Use Sharp Tools:** Just as you would want a sharp knife for precise cooking, sharp tools are essential for harvesting. Dull tools can cause rough cuts, potentially harming the plant and making it vulnerable to diseases. Use pruners for thicker stems or scissors for delicate shoots. Ensure your tool is sharp for a clean, stress-free cut.

- **Try the Pinching Technique:** A simple pinching technique is ideal for softer-stemmed herbs like basil or mint. By using your thumb and forefinger, you can gently pinch off leaves or shoots. This method is not only tender on the plant but also allows for quick and precise harvesting, especially when you only need a small amount.

Post-Harvest Care

After you have harvested your herbs, the care does not stop there. Proper post-harvest treatment ensures you maximize the benefits and longevity of your bounty.

- **Drying:** A method to preserve many herbs. To do it right, lay them out evenly in a well-ventilated area away from direct sunlight. Using drying racks can elevate the herbs, allowing for better airflow, or you can hang them in bunches upside down. Sunlight can rob herbs of their vibrant color and beneficial properties, so a shaded spot is essential.
- **Freezing:** Not all herbs take well to drying. For herbs like parsley or chives, which can lose flavor or medicinal potency when dried, freezing is the way to go. A handy method is to chop the herbs, place them in ice cube trays filled with water, and pop them into the freezer.
- **Storing:** Proper storage is the next step once your herbs are processed and ready. Dark glass jars are ideal as they block sunlight, which can degrade the herbs. Ensure the lids are tight-sealing to keep out moisture and potential contaminants, ensuring your herbs stay fresh and potent for as long as possible.

CHAPTER 6

Mental and Spiritual Healing

For millennia, Native Americans have harnessed the gifts of nature to support well-being, not just physically but mentally and spiritually as well. In this chapter, you will discover time-honored herbs to soothe the mind, uplift the mood, and deepen the soul's connection to nature. You will explore herbs renowned for their stress-alleviating benefits and how they can promote restful sleep. Beyond this, you will also examine spiritual rituals and practices involving sacred plants that provide pathways to personal visions, ancestral wisdom, and enhanced lucidity when sleeping.

Herbs for the Mind

Nature has blessed people with countless gifts, including herbs that hold the power to heal the body and mind. Native American traditions have long revered the natural world, identifying herbs that can restore mental balance and enhance spiritual well-being.

Three categories of herbs address various mental and spiritual needs: *stress relief, mood enhancement,* and *sleep promotion.*

Stress Relievers

Stress, if unchecked, can affect your mental, emotional, and physical well-being. *But did you know that nature offers remedies for these modern-day strains?*

Modern life comes with stress, but it need not dominate your well-being. The wonders of herbs, especially those cherished in Native American traditions, can provide solace and relief to the mind grappling with daily pressures.

The Science Behind Herbal Stress Relief

Herbs like chamomile, lavender, and skullcap contain compounds that interact with our brain and nervous system. For instance, chamomile has apigenin, a compound that binds to specific receptors in the brain, promoting relaxation. Similarly, the aromatic compounds in lavender are known to impact the limbic system, our emotional center, leading to calm. Understanding this science underscores the profound connection between nature and your well-being.

The Synergistic Effect

Combining certain herbs can often compound or synergistically affect stress relief. A blend of chamomile and lavender, for instance, can give a calming experience that is more potent than using each herb individually. This synergy is a testament to the holistic approach Native Americans took toward herbal remedies, understanding that nature's ingredients often work better in concert.

Adapting to Modern Stressors

While the nature of stressors has evolved, the body's response remains rooted in ancient reactions. Today, you might not face the same challenges as your ancestors, but your body's fight-or-flight response to stress remains the same. Incorporating herbs into daily routines—*through teas, baths, or aromatic diffusers*—bridges age-old wisdom and contemporary needs. Making these herbs a part of your lifestyle allows you to create a sanctuary of calm amidst the whirlwind of modern life.

Mindfulness and Herbs

Using herbs for stress relief is not limited to consumption, as it is also about the ritual. The act of brewing a cup of chamomile tea, for example, can be a mindful exercise. Embracing the aroma, observing the infusion, and taking slow sips can anchor you to the present moment, adding another layer of stress relief. This ritualistic approach mirrors the reverence Native Americans held for the natural world, viewing each herb not just as a remedy but as a spiritual ally.

Other herbs that alleviate stress are listed as follows:

- **Black Cohosh:** Traditionally used by Native Americans to relieve stress and anxiety. Consume it as a tincture or as a tea to help relax the mind and body.
- **Damiana:** A mood-lifting herb. Digest as a tea or in tincture form to brighten your day.
- **Mullein:** Used by Native Americans for its calming and respiratory benefits. Preparing a tea with its leaves can offer relief from stress while promoting clearer breathing, making it easier to focus on the present moment.

- **Lemon Balm:** Although not originally native to America, it has been adopted into Native American herbal medicine for its calming effects. Brewing a cup of lemon balm tea can be a calming ritual, aiding relaxation and mental clarity.
- **Slippery Elm:** Consuming it as tea or a tablet can provide a soothing effect, helping to calm the mind.

Regulating Moods

Mood fluctuations impact every facet of life, from relationships to work performance. While pharmaceutical solutions are readily available, they frequently act as a band-aid, temporarily masking the symptoms without addressing the underlying issues. Often, these medications come with a slew of side effects that sometimes outweigh their benefits.

Reasons to Naturally Regulate Mood

Embracing a natural path to mood regulation is a proactive stance in your health journey. Doing so enables the body to heal and balance itself rather than forcing it into submission with synthetic substances.

Consider regulating your mood naturally to get the following benefits:

- **A Holistic Approach:** Herbs offer a holistic approach to mood regulation, addressing the symptoms and root causes of mood imbalances. Many mood-enhancing herbs, such as rhodiola rosea, are adaptogens, which means they help the body adapt to stress and restore balance. Such a natural adaptation can lead to a more sustained emotional balance compared to the temporary relief provided by synthetic drugs.

- **Fewer Side Effects:** Pharmaceutical drugs might provide quick relief but often come with a list of potential adverse reactions. On the other hand, when used correctly and in the right doses, herbs tend to have gentler effects on the body, reducing the risk of undesirable side effects.

- **Synergy with the Body:** Certain herbs stimulate the production of neurotransmitters like serotonin and dopamine, promoting a natural uplift in the mood without causing drastic spikes or lows.

- **Connection to Nature:** Utilizing herbs for mood regulation fosters a deeper connection to nature. This connection, in itself, has therapeutic value.

- **Cost-Effective and Accessible:** For many, herbs present a cost-effective alternative to expensive medications. Furthermore, they are often more accessible and can be cultivated at home or sourced from local herbalists, making them a sustainable choice for long-term mood management.

- **Encouraging Self-awareness:** Choosing to regulate moods with herbs often involves a journey of self-discovery. Individuals become more attuned to their bodies, recognizing subtle changes in mood and determining which herbs resonate best with their unique constitution.

Mood Regulating Herbs

In times of sadness or lethargy, some herbs can act as a ray of sunshine, lifting spirits and enhancing mood, such as:

- **Oregon Grape:** Its root contains berberine, which has been shown to have antidepressant effects.

- **Skullcap:** A medicinal herb that is particularly effective for anxiety and stress.
- **Yellow Dock:** Traditionally used for its blood-purifying and said to help alleviate feelings of low energy and melancholy.

Sleep Aids

A restful night seems like a distant dream for many, often overshadowed by the demands of modern life and the constant pings of digital devices. Whether it is due to anxiety, stress, or an overstimulated mind, the quest for quality sleep becomes an elusive goal, often leading individuals down the rabbit hole of pharmaceutical sleep aids with potential side effects. *What if there was another way—a more natural, holistic approach that aligns with the body's rhythms rather than artificially inducing sleep?*

Benefits of Better Sleep

A deep, undisturbed sleep is the unsung hero behind optimal health and well-being. Some other benefits of restful sleep are the following:

- **Physical Restoration:** Sleep is the body's repair mode. As you enter the deeper stages of sleep, tissue growth and repair occur, and essential hormones are released for growth and stress regulation. A good night's rest ensures the body can perform these crucial tasks efficiently.
- **Cognitive Function:** *Have you ever noticed that even the simplest tasks seem challenging after a restless night?* Sleep plays a role in memory consolidation, problem-solving, and attention. Achieving consistent, quality sleep ensures that you remain sharp and alert.

- **Emotional Well-being:** Emotional resilience is closely tied to your sleep patterns. Consistent restful sleep aids in regulating mood swings, reducing the risk of depression, and promoting an overall sense of happiness.
- **Immune Boost:** Sleep strengthens our immune system. By optimizing your sleep with the help of herbs, you are better equipped to fend off illnesses, making you less susceptible to common colds or viruses.
- **Longevity:** There is a reason why sleep deprivation is used as a form of torture. Chronic lack of sleep can lead to severe health issues such as obesity, diabetes, and heart disease. Prioritizing sleep increases one's lifespan.

Herbs to Aid Sleep

Herbs to lull you into a restorative sleep are listed as follows:

- **Hawthorn:** Popular for its cardiovascular benefits. Such herb also has calming properties to help prepare the body for sleep. A cup of hawthorn tea before bedtime may encourage relaxation and ease you into a restful state.
- **Yarrow:** Contains a mild sedative effect that can alleviate sleeplessness. Its calming impact on the nervous system makes it a helpful herb for those needing a tranquil night.
- **Lemon Balm:** With a delightful citrus aroma, lemon balm reduces stress and anxiety— frequent contributors to sleep issues.
- **Red Clover:** While primarily recognized for its role in women's health, its mild sedative properties further help you wind down at the end of the day, promoting a restful sleep environment.

Soulful Connections

There are various ways in which spiritual rituals, herbs used in divination, and connections to ancestors can facilitate mental and spiritual healing.

Spiritual Rituals

In the context of Native American healing, spiritual rituals are carefully designed sequences of actions aimed at achieving mental, emotional, and spiritual balance. Rituals have a transformative effect on the emotional and psychological state of participants. Engaging in a ceremony often acts as a form of emotional release, allowing individuals to express feelings that might otherwise remain internalized. These ceremonies foster social cohesion.

When you engage in a ritual, you participate in a collective act that enhances communal ties. People feel more connected to each other when they share meaningful experiences, thereby building trust and a sense of belonging. On an individual level, rituals can catalyze significant personal transformation. Such a ceremony offers a structured environment to explore different facets of your identity and spirituality.

Examples of Rituals and Their Significance

These rituals often utilize various elements—*like herbal medicines, natural structures, and specific sequences of actions*—to create transformative experiences. Explore two exemplary rituals: the *sweat lodge ceremony* and the *vision quest*.

Sweat Lodge Ceremony

In this ceremony, participants enter a dome-shaped hut and experience intense heat in the presence of herbal medicines like sage. This process serves as a metaphorical rebirth, a chance to shed negative energies and make room for positivity and growth.

Herbs like sage, cedar, and sweetgrass are essential to this ritual. Sage is often used for smudging, a practice where its leaves are burned, and the smoke is used to purify the participants and the space. Cedar and sweetgrass may be laid on the heated stones to release their essence into the steam, filling the lodge with aromatic and therapeutic properties.

A typical sweat lodge ceremony consists of four rounds, each focusing on *forgiveness, gratitude,* or *healing,* and lasts about 15 to 20 minutes. Songs, drumming, and prayers usually accompany each round, and the Firekeeper brings in fresh, hot stones at the beginning of each one.

The Vision Quest

For vision quest, individuals isolate themselves in nature for an extended period, often four days and nights, without food and sometimes even water. The purpose is to seek visions or guidance from the spiritual realm. Sage might be used to clear the space where the person will sit, while tobacco could be offered to the spirits as a gift.

Unlike the community-based sweat lodge ceremony, the vision quest is a solitary experience. Participants choose a spot in nature, often marked by a circle of stones, to spend time fasting and meditating. Sometimes, an elder or spiritual guide will assist in preparing and interpreting the quest but will not participate directly.

Tobacco is frequently used in vision quests as an offering to the spiritual world. It is considered a sacred plant and is often placed in a small pouch with other meaningful items to serve as a focus during meditation and prayer.

Divination

Divination is a practice often shrouded in mystery, leaving many curious about its true essence. In Native American traditions, divination is a spiritual exercise to gain insights, wisdom, or guidance through various methods, often involving herbs. This practice serves as a tool for individuals to connect with higher powers, ancestors, or spiritual entities to seek answers or enlightenment about health, relationships, or personal challenges.

Various herbs like mugwort, wormwood, and yarrow are often used in divination practices. The herbs are usually burned, and the smoke is believed to carry one's prayers to the spiritual world. Alternatively, some tribes use a method where the herbs are thrown into a fire, and the resulting patterns of smoke or flame are interpreted.

The Role of Herbs in Divination

Herbs are integral in divining practices, serving as the medium through spiritual communication. For example, mugwort is often used for its dream-enhancing qualities; it is believed that burning it before sleep can result in dreams that offer important messages or guidance. Wormwood, on the other hand, has traditionally been used for its psychoactive properties to facilitate trance states, making spiritual contact more accessible.

Interpretation of Signs

The interpretation of the signs or messages received during divination varies from tribe to tribe and individual to individual. This process is usually guided by experienced elders or shamans with deep knowledge of the specific cultural and spiritual contexts. These elders help decode the symbols, smoke patterns, or other messages into actionable insights or spiritual guidance.

Connecting to Ancestors

By honoring the people who came before you, you gain insights into your life's purpose, family history, and personal and spiritual development.

Ways to Connect

People connect with their ancestors in various ways—sometimes by visiting ancestral lands or through rituals involving offerings, prayers, or meditative practices. These rituals also use herbs to honor and communicate with the ancestors.

For instance, tobacco is often used as an offering to show respect and acknowledge the wisdom and sacrifices of those who came before. Similarly, sage is commonly used for purification and as a vessel to carry prayers to the spiritual realm. Burning sage clears negative energies, making the space conducive for spiritual communication. These herbs serve as a bridge, amplifying and channeling your intent into a focused, spiritual connection with your ancestors.

The Healing Power of Ancestral Connections

Actively engaging with ancestral wisdom gives a sense of empowerment and spiritual grounding that is difficult to achieve otherwise. It can be a deeply healing experience, helping you make sense of personal struggles and challenges.

Sacred Herbs

Sacred plants, revered and integrated into various rituals and traditions, play an essential role in mental and spiritual healing. Some examples include the following:

Dream Inducers

For Native American tribes, dreams are a portal to the spiritual world, offering messages and insights. Dream-inducing plants assist in making these dreams more vivid and meaningful.

One of the most revered dream inducers is **calea zacatechichi**, often termed the *"dream herb."* When consumed, it is believed to intensify dreams and make them more lucid. Native tribes used it as a medium to receive spiritual messages and gain clarity on various issues.

Another plant, **mugwort**, is cherished for its dream-promoting properties and ability to drive away evil spirits and ensure protection during the dream journey.

Dream inducers bridge the subconscious, allowing you to venture into the dream world with a heightened awareness and understanding. Through these plants, you can receive guidance and messages that resonate with your spiritual path.

Visionary Herbs

If dream inducers are the gateways to the dream world, visionary herbs unlock spiritual experiences while awake. These herbs offer glimpses of alternate realities and deeper self-awareness. Below are common examples of visionary herbs.

- *Peyote* is a small cactus revered by tribes such as the Huichol and Native American Church for its hallucinogenic properties. When consumed, it offers a spiritual journey filled with vibrant visions and profound introspection.
- *Salvia divinorum*, or the *"sage of the seers,"* is a herb that, when smoked or chewed, can induce intense, albeit short-lived, visionary experiences. Native tribes respect it for its power to connect the spirit to the universe, revealing truths that often lie hidden.

Safe Spiritual Use

Understand that these sacred plants are not recreational substances. They demand respect and should be used with care, ensuring physical and spiritual safety. Follow these tips to ensure the safe use of these herbs.

- **Intent:** Before you delve into the world of sacred plants, set a clear intention. Understand why you are embarking on this journey and what you wish to achieve.
- **Guidance:** It is wise to seek guidance from knowledgeable elders or practitioners, especially for the uninitiated, to understand dosages, preparation methods, and what to expect.

- **Setting:** Ensure you are in a safe, comfortable environment. A supportive, understanding company further enhances the experience.
- **Listen to Your Body:** Every individual reacts differently. If something does not feel right, it is okay to step back. Remember, it is not about chasing an experience but understanding and growing.

Exercise: Mindful Herbal Tea Ritual

Through intentional brewing and mindful sipping, cultivate an enhanced awareness of your inner state, harnessing the transformative powers of selected herbs for mental rejuvenation and spiritual grounding. By merging the ancient art of herbalism with mindfulness practices, this exercise encourages a holistic approach to mental and spiritual well-being.

Materials:

- A herbal tea of your choice *(preferably from the chapter, such as a known stress reliever, mood enhancer, or sleep aid)*
- A teapot or a cup
- Hot water
- A quiet space
- *Optional: a journal and a pen*

Steps:

1. **Preparation:** Choose a herb that resonates with your current emotional or spiritual need. For instance, you might opt for chamomile if you are feeling stressed. If you need to enhance your mood, St. John's wort might be your

choice. Ensure your chosen herb is safe for ingestion and does not interact with any medication you may be on.

2. **Setting the Ambiance**: Find a quiet space where you will not be disturbed. Sit comfortably on a cushion on the floor or in a chair with your feet flat on the ground.

3. **Brewing with Intention**: Hold the herbs as the water heats, and close your eyes. Inhale their aroma deeply. Reflect on the healing properties of the herb and set an intention for this ritual. For example, *"May this chamomile bring calm and peace to my mind."* Pour the hot water over the herbs. As the tea steeps, visualize the water extracting the beneficial properties from the herb.

4. **Mindful Sipping**: Once your tea has steeped adequately, hold the cup with both hands and feel its warmth. Before taking the first sip, smell the aroma deeply and connect with its essence. With every sip, allow the herbal benefits to flow through you, nourishing and healing.

5. **Reflection and Grounding**: After finishing your tea, place your hands on your heart. Take a few deep breaths, expressing gratitude for the herbs and their healing properties. If you have a journal, write down any sensations, emotions, or thoughts that came up during the ritual. This practice helps in grounding the experience and recognizing any subtle shifts in your mental or spiritual state.

6. **Concluding the Ritual**: Thank the herb and the universe for the experience. Clean up your space, and as you do, imagine that you are sealing in the benefits of the ritual, ensuring the healing continues even after it is concluded.

Chapter 7

Family-Centric Herbal Care

Family is the foundation of life for many, and caring for loved ones is a core priority. This chapter explores how herbs can nurture wellness throughout all stages of life. The herbs shared in this chapter cater to age-specific needs, harnessing nature's healing gifts. Sustain your family's health by tapping into centuries of indigenous botanical knowledge.

For Children

The herbal traditions of Native Americans have served families for countless generations. These natural remedies are passed down, holding remedies for every age group.

Infant Care

Infants, with their delicate systems and developing bodies, require specialized care that honors their unique needs. While the modern world offers a range of treatments, there is a long-standing tradition of using nature's offerings for nurturing the youngest. Listed below are different beneficial herbs for infants and some to avoid using on them.

Herbs Beneficial for Infants:

- **Chamomile:** As mentioned, chamomile is not just an adult's bedtime drink. Its calming properties relieve infantile colic fussiness and even induce a calming sleep. A diluted chamomile tea or a gentle massage with chamomile-infused oil can work wonders.
- **Fennel:** A herb to alleviate symptoms of gas and discomfort in babies. A few drops of cooled fennel tea can be given to infants to provide relief.
- **Lavender:** A drop or two of lavender essential oil in a diffuser or a diluted massage can provide relaxation.
- **Calendula:** Ideal for skin issues like diaper rash or minor skin irritations, calendula ointments or creams can be gently applied to the affected areas.

Herbs to Avoid or Use with Caution for Infants:

- **Eucalyptus:** While helpful for respiratory issues in adults, eucalyptus oil might be too strong for infants and lead to breathing difficulties.
- **Peppermint:** Too intense for infants, particularly in oil form. Always dilute it significantly if you must use it.
- **St. John's Wort:** Often used for mood disorders in adults, but may have adverse effects if administered to infants.

Toddler Ailments

Parents often look for natural ways to support their toddler's health, especially when dealing with common issues like tummy troubles, skin irritations, sleep disturbances, and respiratory issues. Incorporating herbs can offer a gentle, effective approach to managing these concerns, nurturing your toddler's well-being with the healing power of nature. Some of the most common issues that herbs can help with are the following:

Tummy Troubles

Toddlers often exhibit signs of digestive discomfort in various ways. They might frequently touch their stomach, become unusually fussy, or even refuse food. Some toddlers may pass gas more than usual or have irregular bowel movements. In these cases, **peppermint** can ease the discomfort, while *fennel seeds,* renowned for their digestive benefits, can be brewed into a tea to help alleviate gas and bloating. **Ginger**, a warming herb, can be introduced in small amounts, especially if the toddler seems nauseous or has motion sickness.

Skin Scrapes and Rashes

Active toddlers often come home with minor scrapes or complain of itchy skin. Redness, swelling, or tiny bumps on the skin can indicate irritations or reactions to insect bites. *Calendula*, with its natural anti-inflammatory properties, can be applied as a salve or lotion to hasten the healing of these minor wounds. *Aloe vera* is a godsend for those unexpected sunburns or skin irritations, providing instant cooling relief. For insect bites or stings that cause itchiness or discomfort, the juice from crushed *plantain leaves* can be a soothing remedy.

Sleep Disturbances

If a toddler frequently wakes up at night, has trouble falling asleep, or seems restless even after a long day of activities, it might indicate sleep disturbances. The calming aroma of **lavender** can help establish a peaceful bedtime routine. A few drops in a diffuser or a diluted massage before bed can work wonders. Similarly, *chamomile* and *lemon balm* teas, known for their sleep-inducing properties, can be diluted to ease the transition into sleep.

Respiratory Support

Wheezing, consistent coughing, or a runny nose can signify a toddler's need for respiratory support. *Mullein* has traditionally been used to address such issues, with mild tea as a soothing cough agent. *Elderberry* supports respiratory health. However, always ensure that any elderberry preparation is free from potentially toxic seeds or stems.

Teething Woes

Drooling, swollen gums, and a marked increase in biting or chewing behaviors can all be signs of a teething toddler. The pain and discomfort can sometimes be overwhelming for them. *Clove*, recognized for its numbing properties, can offer relief. A properly diluted clove oil can be rubbed sparingly on the gums to provide temporary relief.

Safety for Kids

Even though herbal remedies harness nature's power, using them judiciously, especially with children, is crucial. Here are some tips for ensuring safety for kids when using herbal remedies.

- **Recognizing Age-appropriate Herbs:** Just as certain medicines are age-specific, not all herbs suit kids. For instance, herbs like comfrey, used for bone healing in adults, might not be suitable for children due to certain alkaloids present. Always research and ensure that an herb is age-appropriate.

- **Storage and Accessibility:** Children's curiosity knows no bounds. Ensure that herbal preparations, dried herbs, and tinctures are stored securely, preferably locked or out of their reach. Being natural does not mean they cannot be harmful if taken in excess or without need.
- **Herbal Interactions:** Know how different herbs interact, especially when administered simultaneously. While combining peppermint and chamomile might be safe, other combinations might not be. Unless you are well-informed or guided by an expert, it is best to stick to one remedy at a time.
- **Inculcate Respect for Nature:** Education is crucial for older children who might start recognizing plants and herbs. Field trips to nature reserves, where they can see herbs in their natural habitat, can be enlightening. Teaching them about the benefits and dangers of certain plants ensures that they treat nature with reverence and respect.
- **Allergies and Sensitivities:** Just as some kids are allergic to certain foods, they might also react to specific herbs. Always observe for any unusual reactions after introducing a new herbal remedy, like rashes, breathing difficulties, or behavioral changes.

Teen and Adult Care

Regarding health and well-being, the challenges teenagers and adults face can be overwhelming, from the tumultuous years of adolescence marked by hormonal upheavals to the later years of adulthood, characterized by changing life phases. However, Native American herbal traditions provide remedies that have been relied upon for generations.

Hormonal Balance

Hormones are like messengers, directing various physiological processes in your body, from growth and energy production to mood and reproduction. An imbalance can disrupt these processes, leading to various symptoms and ailments. For women, this might manifest as painful menstruations, fertility issues, or menopausal discomforts. For men, it could mean issues like reduced libido, hair loss, or prostate problems. Therefore, achieving and maintaining hormonal balance is vital for overall health and quality of life.

An array of herbs that can be used to support hormonal health. For instance—

- **For Menstrual Health:** Blue cohosh has been traditionally used by Native Americans to address menstrual discomfort and to induce labor during childbirth. Usage needs expert guidance due to its potent nature.
- **Menopause and Beyond:** Wild yam contains diosgenin, a compound that can act similarly to estrogen in the body. It has been used to alleviate symptoms of menopause, like hot flashes and mood disturbances.
- **For the Fellas:** Men, too, face hormonal challenges, particularly as they age. Saw Palmetto, native to the southeastern U.S., has been essential to Native American pharmacopeia. Rich in fatty acids and phytosterols, saw palmetto can support prostate health, potentially easing

symptoms of benign prostatic hyperplasia (BPH) and helping regulate testosterone levels.

Anxiety and Lifestyle

As the pressures of modern living bear down heavily, anxiety has become an unwelcome companion for many. This pervasive stress not only affects mental well-being but has tangible physical repercussions. Prolonged anxiety can lead to sleep disturbances, digestive issues, weakened immunity, and even chronic diseases. While modern medicine often provides temporary relief, turning to nature can offer holistic and lasting solutions.

Herbal remedies work harmoniously with the body, supporting and nourishing it rather than merely suppressing symptoms. They address the root causes, helping to restore natural balance and resilience. Moreover, they typically come with fewer side effects than synthetic medications. Using herbs to manage stress taps into ancient wisdom, harnessing the natural potency of plants to bring about mental tranquility, physical relaxation, and overall wellness.

Below are herbs that restore mental calm, energy, and digestive harmony.

- **Mental Calm:** Passionflower, found primarily in the southeastern parts of the U.S., was traditionally used by Native Americans for its sedative and calming properties. It is believed to increase gamma-aminobutyric acid (GABA) levels in the brain, reducing brain activity and helping individuals relax. If your mind seems in constant turmoil, especially at bedtime, sipping on passionflower tea might offer the mental respite you crave.

- **Energize Without Jitters:** Native Americans have used American ginseng as a restorative tonic for centuries. Unlike the intense caffeine rush, American ginseng offers a steadier, more sustained energy boost, sharpening mental clarity and warding off fatigue.
- **Digestive Harmony:** A troubled mind can lead to a troubled gut. Slippery elm, native to North America, is recognized for its mucilaginous properties. When consumed, it forms a gel-like substance that coats the digestive tract, soothing irritation and inflammation.

Elders' Wellness

Elders, with their wealth of wisdom and experience, have special health requirements. Traditional Native American herbal knowledge offers remedies tailored specifically to these needs.

Age-Related Remedies

As you journey into the golden years, the phrase *"adapting to life phases"* takes profound significance. Beyond the common understanding of age, it encompasses the physical, emotional, and mental changes you undergo. The body might display signs of wear, but these signs are markers of wisdom, experiences lived, and lessons learned.

Address common aging-related ailments with the following:

- **Joint Health:** Age is often accompanied by creaky joints, making simple tasks a chore. But nature provides solace. Beyond the *devil's claw*, the *yucca root* is a beacon of relief. A cornerstone in Native American herbal practices, its rich saponin content soothes inflamed joints and fosters flexibility.

- **Digestive Wellness:** The once strong digestive system may occasionally falter with age. Suddenly, favorite meals might lead to discomfort, or the digestive process may lag. Deeply rooted in Native American traditions, *dandelion root* stimulates digestion. More than that, it ensures that the body effectively absorbs and utilizes nutrients. Thus, every meal becomes a source of nourishment, catering not just to the body but also to the soul.

- **Skin and Vitality:** Age might rob the skin of its youthful elasticity. *Aloe vera* helps support the skin's health. Its hydrating and healing properties ensure that the skin remains supple and radiant. Beyond the aesthetic, aloe also aids in cellular regeneration, ensuring that the elders' vitality shines from within.

CHAPTER 8

Specialized Herbal Formulas

Herbal remedies have been used for centuries to support women's health and well-being. This chapter provides an in-depth look at specialized herbal formulas that can help women navigate key aspects of their lives. From fertility and menstruation to pregnancy and menopause, you will explore how targeted combinations of herbs can offer natural solutions for the female body. The chapter also addresses concerns unique to men's health, such as prostate health, libido, endurance, and sleep issues. You will get tips on crafting customized herbal blends tailored to your needs.

Specialized Herbal Formulas for Women's Health

Women's health encompasses a wide range of issues, from fertility and reproductive support to menstrual and menopausal remedies and pregnancy.

Fertility and Reproductive Support

Certain herbs have been singled out for their potent effects in aiding fertility and supporting the reproductive system.

Herbal Remedies

For generations, Native American women have turned to herbs as effective, natural solutions for various fertility issues, from irregular cycles to hormone imbalances, such as:

- **Red Clover**: Rich in isoflavones, plant-based chemicals that mimic the estrogen hormone. These isoflavones can help balance hormones, which is crucial for women trying to conceive. Native American tribes have often utilized red clover in their herbal preparations for fertility enhancement.
- **Black Cohosh**: Originating from North America, black cohosh is a staple in Native American herbal medicine. It is often used for its potential to regulate menstrual cycles and stimulate ovulation. In the Native American tradition, it is sometimes combined with other herbs to make a potent mixture that aids fertility.
- **Nettle**: Abundant in key nutrients like iron, calcium, and magnesium. These nutrients are essential for preparing a woman's body for conception and a healthy pregnancy. Native American women have traditionally consumed nettle tea for its nutrient-rich profile to support fertility.

Example Formula and How to Use It

For a potent fertility-boosting blend, you can create a herbal tea using the following:

Ingredients:

- 2 parts Red Clover
- 1 part Black Cohosh
- 2 parts Nettle

How to Prepare the Tea:

1. Boil a cup of water and pour it into a teapot with the herbal mixture.
2. Let it steep for about 10 to 15 minutes.
3. Strain and pour into a cup.

Dosage:

Drink this herbal blend two to three times a week for optimal results.

Caution:

As with any natural remedy, it is always a good idea to consult a healthcare provider, especially if you are trying to conceive or are already pregnant.

Menstrual and Menopausal Remedies

The ebbs and flows of hormones during the menstrual cycle and menopause often bring a host of symptoms that range from mildly annoying to debilitating. As discussed in a previous chapter, Native American herbal wisdom offers a variety of solutions to manage these symptoms. Get a more in-depth look below at the herbs traditionally used for these purposes.

Herbal Remedies

These natural remedies can be used for a wide range of issues, from the discomfort of menstrual cramps to the complex hormonal shifts of menopause.

- **Red Clover:** Rich in phytoestrogens, natural plant compounds that mimic estrogen in the body. Native American tribes have traditionally used red clover to manage symptoms of menopause, such as hot flashes and mood swings. The herb can also be used to relieve premenstrual syndrome (PMS) symptoms.
- **Black Cohosh:** Relieve hot flashes, mood swings, and sleep problems, black cohosh is another important herb in Native American medicine. The herb targets the hormonal pathway, offering relief to women going through menopause.
- **Chaste Tree (Vitex):** While not native to America, chaste tree was adopted into Native American herbal practices. It is highly effective in regulating menstrual cycles and relieving PMS symptoms. Native American women have used this herb to treat irregular periods and to alleviate the symptoms of menopause.
- **Mullein:** Used by Native American tribes for various respiratory issues, but it also finds use in women's health. Mullein leaves can be used in a poultice to relieve breast tenderness, a common symptom during the menstrual cycle.

Example Formula and How to Use It

Using these specialized herbal formulas helps navigate the complexities of menstrual and menopausal symptoms with the wisdom of herbs at your disposal. For menopausal relief, brew a tea using:

Ingredients:

- 3 parts sage
- 1 part red clover

How to Prepare the Tea:

1. Boil water and pour it over the herbal mixture.
2. Steep for 10 to 15 minutes.
3. Strain and drink.

Dosage:

Consume once daily to alleviate menopausal symptoms like hot flashes.

Note: Always consult with a healthcare provider before starting any new herbal treatment, especially if you are already taking medications or have a pre-existing medical condition.

Pregnancy Support

Pregnancy is a transformative experience that comes with its own set of joys and challenges. While the excitement of welcoming a new life is unparalleled, the journey also brings various discomforts.

Herbs for Morning Sickness

Natural remedies to ease common morning sickness are listed as follows:

- **Mullein:** Effective remedy for gastrointestinal discomfort, making it a useful herb for conditions like nausea.
- **Black Root:** A powerful laxative and liver cleanser. Helpful remedy for digestive issues, including feelings of sickness or nausea.

Pregnancy-Safe Remedies

Pregnancy can bring a host of other issues like sleeplessness, anxiety, and muscle cramps. Know which herbs are safe to use during this period, as some may not be advisable for expectant mothers.

- **Red Raspberry Leaf:** Tone the uterus, improve labor outcomes, and reduce postpartum bleeding.
- **Nettle:** Rich in iron, calcium, and other vital nutrients, nettle is a powerhouse that helps keep both the mother and baby nourished.
- **Oatstraw:** Contains calcium and magnesium, essential for developing the baby's bones and nervous system. It also helps alleviate stress and anxiety, making it a great companion for expectant mothers.
- **Slippery Elm:** Combat heartburn, a common issue during pregnancy. However, as it is high in calcium, it is best to consult a healthcare provider before using it.

Men's Health

Men also benefit from herbal plants. For instance—

Libido and Prostate

The term *"libido"* refers to sexual desire or drive, while the *"pros-tate"* is a small gland that plays a crucial role in the male reproductive system. Addressing issues related to both is not just a matter of sexual or urinary health but overall well-being. It can affect emotional health, relationships, and self-esteem.

Men often avoid this topic due to feelings of embarrassment or inadequacy. Many men even feel emasculated when facing issues like low libido or prostate problems. However, these are common and natural conditions that many men experience, particularly as they age. There is nothing shameful about wanting to improve in these areas.

Herbs for Prostate and Libido

Improve prostate and libido with the following herbs:

- **Saw Palmetto:** The berries were used to treat urinary issues and reproductive system challenges. Saw palmetto works by inhibiting the conversion of testosterone to dihydrotestosterone (DHT), a hormone that can lead to prostate enlargement. For a mild prostate or libido boost, consider taking 320 mg of saw palmetto extract daily, or consult with your healthcare provider for a personalized dose.

- **Damiana:** Native tribes in the Southwest and Mexico have utilized Damiana leaves for centuries as an aphrodisiac and for treating various sexual disorders. Damiana's compounds are thought to stimulate blood flow to genital areas and boost sexual performance. Damiana can be consumed in a tea form or as a tincture. For a libido-enhancing tea, steep one tablespoon of dried Damiana leaves in hot water for 15 to 20 minutes.

- **Nettle:** Like saw palmetto, nettle root can inhibit the conversion of testosterone to DHT. This herb aids in reducing prostate inflammation and improving urinary flow. Nettle root can be taken as a capsule, tea, or tincture. For prostate support, try consuming 300 to 500 mg daily in capsule form or make a nettle root tea.

Strength and Endurance

Strength and endurance are not merely abstract ideals. In this context, *"strength"* goes beyond mere physical prowess, including resilience and the ability to endure stress or illness. Similarly, *"endurance"* is not only about stamina in physical activities but also signifies a sustained vitality and zest for life. These attributes influence multiple facets of existence, from career success and interpersonal relationships to mental health and overall quality of life.

Some men might avoid discussing these issues, fearing it would make them appear weak or less masculine. Yet, there is no shame in wanting to bolster your strength and endurance. These are integral aspects of a fulfilling, active life. Just as one would work out to keep muscles strong, focusing on strength and endurance through herbal remedies can be a proactive measure for holistic well-being.

Herbs for Strength and Endurance

The following are herbs for enhancing strength and endurance:

- **Sumac:** Native American tribes have long valued sumac for its medicinal benefits, including its use as a tonic to improve stamina and reduce fatigue. The antioxidants in sumac help combat oxidative stress, enhancing overall vitality and energy levels. Sumac berries can be brewed into tea. To boost endurance, consider drinking one cup of sumac tea daily.
- **Yucca:** Used as an anti-inflammatory agent to improve digestive health, which can contribute to overall strength. Yucca's saponins help with nutrient absorption, potentially increasing energy and endurance. It can be consumed in capsule form or as a tincture. Consult your healthcare provider for the right dosage for you.
- **Oregon Grape:** The berberine in Oregon grape has anti-inflammatory and antimicrobial properties that aid muscle recovery. Consume in capsule form or brewed into a tea. Typical dosage ranges from 300 to 500 mg per day in capsule form.

Sleep Issues

Good sleep helps your body repair itself and your mind processes the events of the day. Lack of sleep, or poor-quality sleep, affects everything from cognitive function and mood to cardiovascular health. One issue particularly common among men is snoring, which can be a sign of obstructive sleep apnea, a potentially serious disorder that interrupts regular breathing during sleep. Left unaddressed, sleep issues can escalate into more serious health problems.

Herbs for Sleep

Transform your sleep cycle and achieve the restful nights you deserve with herbs such as:

- **Valerian Root:** Used to treat insomnia, stress, and even headaches. Valerian root contains compounds that interact with neurotransmitters in your brain, telling your body to relax and prepare for sleep. A dose of 300 to 600 mg about 30 minutes before bedtime is often recommended for sleep issues.
- **Hops:** Have a compound called myrcene, which has sedative properties. It works well in synergy with Valerian Root. Try taking a tincture or capsule that combines Hops with Valerian Root for a double-whammy against insomnia. You can also use Hops in a sleep pillow.
- **Lemon Balm:** Native Americans have employed Lemon Balm for various purposes, including aiding sleep and reducing anxiety. It has a calming effect on the nervous system, helping to induce sleep. Make a cup of Lemon Balm tea before bedtime or take it in capsule form. A standard dosage is about 300 mg.

Custom Blends

No two bodies are the same, and what works for one person might not work for another. Learn how to create personalized mixes with the listed tips.

- **Know Your Herbs:** Before diving into blending, it is essential to familiarize yourself with the properties of various herbs. For example, sage is great for hot flashes, while black cohosh improves hormonal balance.

- **Proportions Matter:** Using too much of one herb could overshadow the benefits of others. Start with equal parts of each herb and then adjust based on results.
- **Method of Preparation:** The method you choose can significantly impact the effectiveness of your herbal blend. Teas are great for quick absorption, while tinctures can have a longer shelf life.

Adjusting to Individual Needs

Personalization is the cornerstone of effective herbal treatment. Adjust your herbal blends to meet individual needs by doing the following:

- **Monitoring Effects:** Consider how a blend affects you. Keep a journal to track any symptoms, mood, or overall well-being changes.
- **Consultation and Testing:** Do not shy away from consulting with an herbalist or healthcare provider. These people can provide insights and may even recommend specific tests, such as allergy tests, to ensure you choose the most appropriate herbs.
- **The Adjustment Process:** After tracking effects and consulting a professional, start tweaking your blend. Maybe your sleep blend works, but you wake up groggy. Try reducing the valerian root and adding more lemon balm for a milder effect.

CHAPTER 9

Enhancing Beauty and Vitality

The quest for physical beauty and vitality is not vanity. Think of it as something deeply intertwined with spirituality and the nurturing of one's inner essence. This chapter aims to shed light on some of the most potent Native American herbs used for enhancing skin and hair care, as well as the overall vitality of your body.

Natural Facial Remedies

When it comes to facial care, the temptation to opt for quick, mass-produced solutions is often high. However, many people do not realize that these chemical-laden products often do more harm than good. Native American herbs, in contrast, offer a holistic approach to skincare that has been trusted for centuries. Rich in natural elements and devoid of artificial additives, these herbs are arguably more effective and gentle than their manufactured counterparts.

Sage

For anti-aging, many turn to expensive creams and serums that promise miracles but often underdeliver. Sage is packed with antioxidants that naturally fight off the free radicals causing skin aging. One of the best ways to use sage is through a steam facial. Boil a pot of water and add a handful of sage leaves. Once it is boiled, transfer the water to a bowl. Lean over the bowl and cover your head with a towel, allowing the steam to envelop your face. This process not only helps the skin absorb the beneficial properties of sage but also cleans out the pores.

Yarrow

Substitute your toner with yarrow. Most commercial toners are alcohol-based, which can strip your skin of its natural oils and worsen your acne issues. Yarrow, on the other hand, has natural astringent properties without the harshness of alcohol. To make a yarrow face wash or toner, boil a teaspoon of dried yarrow leaves in a cup of water. Allow it to cool down, and then strain the liquid. Soak a cotton ball in this yarrow infusion and gently apply it to your face, focusing on acne-prone areas. Besides its astringent qualities, yarrow has anti-inflammatory and antiseptic properties, making it a triple threat against acne. It reduces redness, fights off bacteria, and helps tighten your pores for a clearer complexion.

Hair Growth Boosters

Hair issues are as varied as the people who experience them. From dandruff and dryness to hair thinning and premature graying, each problem is a unique challenge. Hair thinning and loss are frequently associated with hormonal imbalances, genetics, or inadequate nutrition. Dandruff typically stems from an oily scalp, subpar hygiene practices, or fungal infections. Many experience dry and frizzy hair due to insufficient moisture, which certain weather conditions or harsh haircare products can worsen. Premature graying is mostly genetic, although stress and poor nutrition can hasten its onset. Lastly, split ends often arise from a moisture deficiency or the consistent use of heat-styling appliances.

Usually, you seek quick fixes like over-the-counter shampoos or prescription medications, but these often come with side effects and only treat symptoms rather than the underlying issue. Native American herbs offer a rich reservoir of natural solutions for these common hair problems, promoting growth and contributing to overall hair health.

Nettle

Nettle has vitamins A and C and minerals like iron and magnesium. Most chemical shampoos offer a quick fix but might strip your hair of its natural oils, making it dry and brittle. Nettle, on the other hand, nourishes your hair from root to tip.

Stepping dried nettle leaves in hot water for 10 to 15 minutes to create a nettle tea rinse. Strain the leaves and let the liquid cool. After your regular shampoo, pour the nettle tea over your hair, ensuring it covers all areas, and massage it into your scalp. Rinse with cold water.

Saw Palmetto

The hormone dihydrotestosterone (DHT) is often the culprit behind hair thinning and loss, especially in men. Prescription medications like finasteride do inhibit DHT but can come with side effects like sexual dysfunction. Saw palmetto is a natural DHT blocker with far fewer side effects.

Saw palmetto is usually in oil form or as a supplement. If you use the oil, apply it to your scalp and massage gently. Leave it on for at least 30 minutes before washing off. If you take it as a supplement, consult a healthcare provider for the appropriate dosage.

Rosemary

Rosemary stands out for its high antioxidant content, which can improve blood circulation to the scalp, thereby promoting hair growth. Unlike many silicone-based hair products that offer only an illusion of shine, rosemary nourishes your hair for a natural luster.

Warm a few tablespoons of rosemary oil and massage it into your scalp. Leave it on for 30 to 40 minutes before washing it off with a mild shampoo. You can also add a few drops of rosemary oil to your regular hair oil for an added boost.

Herbal Baths and Scrubs

Taking a bath is often considered a quick way to get clean and refreshed, *but what if it could be more than that? What if it could be an experience that cleanses and heals?* Native American herbal practices take the bathing ritual to a holistic level. These baths and scrubs can turn your bathroom into a spa, from detoxifying the skin to boosting the immune system.

Black Walnut and Echinacea

Black walnut is known for its antiseptic and cleansing properties, while echinacea boosts the immune system and has anti-inflammatory benefits.

Step-by-Step Guide

1. **Gather What You Need.**
   - ○ 2 tablespoons of black walnut hull powder and 2 tablespoons of dried echinacea.
2. **Preparation**: Mix the black walnut hull powder and dried echinacea in a bowl.
3. **Brew**: Boil the mixture in a pot with 2 to 3 cups of water for about 10 minutes.
4. **Use**: Strain and add the liquid to your bathwater. Soak for at least 20 minutes to allow the herbs to detoxify your skin.

Mint and Yucca

Mint provides a refreshing scent and has natural antibacterial properties. Yucca root is rich in saponins, which have natural cleansing abilities, making it a good choice for a scrub.

Step-by-Step Guide

1. **Gather What You Need**: A handful of fresh mint leaves and 2 tablespoons of yucca root powder.
2. **Preparation**: Crush the mint leaves in a mortar and pestle to release the oils. Mix the crushed mint with the yucca root powder.
3. **Use**: Apply the scrub to damp skin in circular motions, focusing on areas that need more attention, like elbows or knees.
4. **Rinse**: Wash off with warm water.

Weight Management

Explore how certain herbs can act as appetite suppressants and metabolism boosters, offering you a holistic approach to weight management.

Appetite Suppressants

Appetite suppressants are substances that help control your hunger by sending signals to your brain that you are full, which ultimately aids in reducing food intake. Some herbs that serve as natural appetite suppressants include the following:

Yerba Mate

A traditional South American herb that has found its way into Native American herbal practices. Consumed mainly as a tea, it not only suppresses your appetite but also boosts your energy levels. Yerba mate contains special compounds that interact with your hunger hormones, signaling to your brain that you are satiated. Hence, you eat less and make better food choices, contributing to weight management. To prepare, boil a cup of water and add yerba mate leaves. Allow them to steep for about 5 to 10 minutes. Strain and drink this tea approximately 30 minutes before your meals.

Prickly Pear

A type of cactus that is fiber-abundant and traditionally used in Native American communities to curb hunger. Consume the fruit of the prickly pear cactus directly, or if you prefer, it is also available in capsule form. Take it as directed on the packaging or by your healthcare provider. The high fiber content in prickly pear acts like a sponge in your stomach, absorbing water and expanding. Such content provides a fuller feeling for longer, reducing the likelihood of overeating.

Metabolism Boosters

After diving into appetite suppressants, shift your focus to metabolism boosters. *But what exactly is metabolism?* In simple terms, metabolism is the chemical process in your body that converts food into energy. The faster your metabolism, the more calories you burn, making losing or maintaining a healthy weight easier.

The following are herbs and natural ingredients that can help give your metabolism a little nudge.

Cayenne Pepper

Cayenne pepper is not just a pantry staple for adding heat to your dishes. This herb boosts metabolism, aiding in faster calorie burning. Add a small pinch of cayenne pepper to your meals for a spicy kick. Mix a pinch into a glass of lemon water for a palatable approach, and drink it in the morning. Cayenne pepper contains an active component called capsaicin. Capsaicin has thermogenic effects, meaning it can help increase your body temperature. As your body works to cool itself down, it burns more calories, increasing your metabolic rate.

Ginger

Although Native American cultures have widely embraced native to Southeast Asia, ginger has many health benefits, including its ability to speed up metabolism. Ginger is a natural thermogenic, meaning it can increase your body temperature. When your body has to work harder to return to its normal temperature, it uses more energy, which means you burn more calories. To use, grate fresh ginger root and add it to your meals, or for a comforting beverage, prepare a warm ginger tea. Boil a cup of water, add sliced ginger root, and let it simmer for 10 minutes before straining.

Detoxification

"Detoxification" is often associated with trendy juice cleanses and detox teas. However, the essence of detoxification is rooted in consuming natural food, including herbs, such as:

Liver-Cleansing Herbs

A healthy liver can filter out toxins and waste more efficiently. *But what if you could give it a natural boost?* Herbs offer powerful ways to do just that. Get to know some of these liver-cleansing wonders better below.

Milk Thistle

Milk thistle is a go-to herb for liver health, as it acts like a shield, protecting your liver cells from damage. It also aids in the regeneration of new liver cells. So, think of milk thistle as a daily multivitamin for your liver. When using milk thistle, you have two options. Brew a milk thistle tea with a teaspoon of the seeds in boiling water for 10 minutes. Alternatively, you can find milk thistle in tincture or capsule forms at your local health store.

Dandelion Root

While most people consider dandelion a pesky weed, it is a liver-cleansing gem. Dandelion root packs a punch when it comes to liver health. Rich in antioxidants, it helps neutralize harmful free radicals. Additionally, it stimulates bile production, which aids in digesting fats and absorbing essential nutrients. Try brewing dandelion root into a tea, or take it in supplement form. Add a teaspoon of the root to boiling water for tea and let it steep for about 10 minutes.

Kidney Detoxifiers

The kidneys are the unsung heroes of detoxification. These bean-shaped organs are biological filters that remove waste products, balance electrolytes, and regulate blood pressure. However, much like the liver, kidneys can become burdened due to poor diet, medications, or exposure to environmental toxins. When this happens, they cannot operate at their optimal capacity, which can lead to health issues like urinary tract infections, kidney stones, or even chronic kidney disease.

Detoxify your kidney with the listed herbs:

Nettle

Steep nettle leaves in boiling water for 10 minutes to prepare a nutrient-rich tea. Incorporating this powerful herb into your daily routine is a simple way. Nettle acts as a natural diuretic, which means it helps facilitate increased urine production. This action is beneficial for flushing out toxins from the kidneys and preventing the formation of kidney stones. Furthermore, it is packed with antioxidants that provide extra protection to the kidneys.

Juniper Berries

Juniper berries are known for their natural diuretic properties. They stimulate the kidneys, enhancing their ability to eliminate waste and excess bodily fluids. The berries' detoxifying properties can thus aid in keeping the kidneys functioning optimally. Juniper berries can be brewed into tea by steeping in hot water for 10 minutes or so. Alternatively, they are also available in capsule form for those who prefer a quick and convenient option.

Conclusion

In a rapidly changing world filled with quick fixes and fleeting moments, this book has anchored you back to the timeless embrace of nature and the profound traditions of Native American herbalism. As you journeyed through the pages, you encountered the meticulous art of cultivating a healing garden—understanding the life cycles of plants and the harmonious interplay of soil, water, and sunlight. Moreover, this book unraveled the relationship between nutrition and herbs, emphasizing that true healing is not just about alleviating physical ailments. It is a more nuanced ballet of consuming the right foods synergized with potent herbs while nourishing the spirit through meditations and mindfulness practices.

As modernity brings forth challenges, often disconnecting us from our roots and the rhythms of nature, this guide has served as a bridge. A bridge that not only spans across time, reconnecting you to ancient wisdom, and skillfully integrates this wisdom into the demands and intricacies of today's world.

The goal of this book was to offer you more than just facts and remedies. It was to provide a holistic compass, guiding you not just in physical healing but also in emotional and spiritual transformation. And as you have navigated through its chapters, you have been equipped with tools and insights, fulfilling that promise.

As you move forward, remember that true wellness and balance stem from a deep, harmonious connection with nature and the age-old wisdom of our predecessors. Let this be your guiding light, leading you toward a life steeped in health, tranquility, and meaning. Cherish this knowledge, and let it illuminate your path as you forge ahead, crafting a future rich in authenticity and purpose.

Techniques Recap

The following techniques are found in *"Lost Native American Herbalist's Secrets [All in 1]:"*

#	Technique/ Tip	Explanation
1	Ensure herb purity	Use herbs free from pesticides and contaminants.
2	Source from reputable suppliers or grow your own	Choose reliable sources or consider growing your own herbs for quality and efficacy.
3	Learn about each herb	Understand taste, aroma, and health benefits of each herb to determine its suitability.
4	Be aware of herb side effects	Even beneficial herbs can have side effects, especially in large quantities or with other herbs or medications.
5	Avoid combining herbs without knowledge	Do not combine herbs or use them in large amounts without proper knowledge.
6	Research and consult experts	Always research and consult experts when dealing with potent herbs.
7	Consult healthcare professional for medication	Consult a healthcare professional before adding new herbs to your regimen, especially if you're taking medications.
8	Start with smaller doses	Begin with smaller doses to gauge individual reactions since everyone's body is different.

#	Technique/ Tip	Explanation
9	Extract essence with hot water	Place leaves, stems, or roots in hot water to extract the essence of the plant.
10	Experiment with unconventional pairings	Be open to unconventional herb and food combinations for unique and nutritious dishes.
11	Invest in a field guide for plant identification	If you explore outdoors or forage, invest in a field guide for accurate plant identification.
12	Join plant identification workshops	Participate in workshops on plant identification and herbal preparations for hands-on experience and knowledge sharing.
13	Be cautious with wild harvesting	Refrain from wild harvesting until confident in distinguishing between edible and harmful look-alike plants.
14	Perform a taste test for uncertain safety	If uncertain about a plant's safety, perform a taste test to ensure it's safe for consumption.
15	Photograph unknown plants for identification	Take clear photographs of unfamiliar plants for later identification by experts or online resources.
16	Gradually adapt to new herbal beverages	When trying new herbal beverages, start with weaker brews and gradually increase strength as you become accustomed.
17	Observe changes after herbal consumption	Pay attention to changes in how you feel after consuming herbs, whether positive or negative, and adjust accordingly.
18	Keep a record of herb usage and effects	Note down the herb's name, quantity, brewing time, and effects to refine your herbal routine.

#	Technique/ Tip	Explanation
19	Stay updated on herb information	Regularly update your knowledge of herbs, especially those known to cause allergies.
20	Track experiences with herbs	Record each herb consumed, quantity, date, and any reactions to identify patterns or herbs that may not suit your system.
21	Seek medical help for severe reactions	If you experience severe reactions like difficulty breathing or chest pain, contact emergency services and inform them about the herb consumed.
22	Consult a healthcare provider for allergies	If you have allergies or are on medications, consult a healthcare provider, preferably one knowledgeable about herbal remedies, before using new herbs.
23	Harvest responsibly	Harvest only a small fraction of plants to allow the majority to mature, seed, and replenish.
24	Promote regrowth after root harvesting	After harvesting roots, consider sowing seeds of the same plant in the vicinity to support regrowth and ecological balance.
25	Express gratitude through offerings	Leave offerings as a symbol of gratitude to maintain a balanced cycle of giving and taking.
26	Minimize moisture loss during hand watering	Aim water close to the roots to minimize moisture loss through evaporation.
27	Be cautious with herb dosage and side effects	Using herbs in the correct doses tends to have gentler effects on the body and reduces the risk of undesirable side effects.

#	Technique/ Tip	Explanation
28	Use pinching technique for softer-stemmed herbs	When harvesting softer-stemmed herbs like basil or mint, use a pinching technique for gentle leaf or shoot removal.
29	Dry herbs in a well-ventilated area	To dry herbs, lay them out evenly in a well-ventilated area away from direct sunlight or use drying racks for better airflow.
30	Freeze herbs in ice cube trays	Chop herbs, place them in ice cube trays filled with water, and freeze for convenient storage.
31	Store herbs in dark glass jars	Use dark glass jars with tight-sealing lids to block sunlight and keep herbs fresh and potent.
32	Monitor reactions after herbal remedies	Be watchful for unusual reactions like rashes, breathing difficulties, or behavioral changes after trying a new herbal remedy.
33	Balance herb quantities for maximum benefits	Avoid using too much of one herb, as it can overshadow the benefits of others. Start with equal parts and adjust as needed.

References

Aiyana Henhawk. (2021). *Native American Herbal Remedies: Traditional Herbal Remedies & Recipes to Heal Common Ailments.* Tony Alex Ventimiglia.

Alfred Savinelli. (2002). *Plants of Power: Native American Ceremony and the Use of Sacred Plants.* Native Voices.

Alma R. Hutchens. (1991). *Indian Herbalogy of North America: The Definitive Guide to Native Medicinal Plants and Their Uses.* Shambhala Publications.

Alma R. Hutchens. (1992). *A Handbook of Native American Herbs: The Pocket Guide to 125 Medicinal Plants and Their Uses.* Shambhala Publications.

Anthony J. Cichoke. (2001). *Secrets of Native American Herbal Remedies: A Comprehensive Guide to the Native American Tradition of Using Herbs and the Mind/Body/Spirit Connection for Improving Health and Well-being.* Penguin.

Cheyenne Allen. (2021). *Native American Herbalism: Ancient Wisdom and Herbal Tradition for Radiant Health. The Ultimate Herbalist Bible 4 BOOKS in 1: All You Need to Know from the Heart of Nature to Your Apothecary Table.* Independently Published.

Francine Milford, BS, LMT, CTN. (2018). *The Aromatherapy Massage A Guide to Facial Massage.* Lulu.com.

Gurtu, Amulya. (2019). *Intellectual Property Rights and the Protection of Traditional Knowledge.* Dewani, Nisha Dhanraj. IGI Global.

Ina Vandebroek. (2009). *Traveling Cultures and Plants: The Ethnobiology and Ethnopharmacy of Human Migrations.* Andrea Pieroni. Berghahn Books.

Kenneth S. Cohen. (2018). *Honoring the Medicine: The Essential Guide to Native American Healing.* Random House Publishing Group.

Kristiina A. Vogt. (2020). *The Medicine Wheel: Environmental Decision-Making Process of Indigenous Peoples.* Michael E. Marchand. MSU Press.

M. Kat Anderson. (2005). *Tending the Wild: Native American Knowledge and the Management of California's Natural Resources.* University of California Press.

Makawee Huaman. (2021). *Native American Encyclopedia of Herbal Medicine: 5 Books In 1: The Best Remedies Used by Native Americans for Hundreds of Years. Herbs from Gardening to Storage, Their Uses and Recipes to Treat Kids.* Independently Published.

Naira Adahi. (2021). *Introduction to Native American Culture: A Complete Guide to the Culture of Native Americans.* Florin Ovidiu Burca.

Natasha Cippewa. (2021). *Native American Herbal Apothecary: The Complete Guide to Herbalism. Learn How to Heal Common Ailments with Herbal Remedies and How to Replace Classical Medicine to Improve Your Wellness.* Independently Published.

Pamela Hirsch. (2000). *Planting the Future: Saving Our Medicinal Herbs*. Rosemary Gladstar. Inner Traditions / Bear & Co.

Rosemary Kennedy. (2021). *Native American Herbalism Bible 1: THE FORGOTTEN BOOK TO TRADITIONAL HERBS OF NORTH AMERICA TO HELP AND IMPROVE YOUR WELLNESS*. Rosemary Kennedy.

Sean Sherman. (2017). *The Sioux Chef's Indigenous Kitchen*. U of Minnesota Press.

Sissi Wachtel-Galor. (2011). *Herbal Medicine: Biomolecular and Clinical Aspects, Second Edition*. Iris F. F. Benzie. CRC Press.

Steven Foster. (1995). *Forest Pharmacy: Medicinal Plants in American Forests*. Forest History Society.

Tallulah Greyeyes. (2021a). *Native American Herbalist's Bible: 6 BOOKS. a Modern Guide to Traditional Native American Herbalism to Embrace a New Way of Living. Dispensatory, Recipes, and Remedies for Everyday Health | Includes the Spiritual History and Treatments for Kids*. Independently Published.

Tallulah Greyeyes. (2021b). *Native American Herbal Apothecary: 3 BOOKS in 1 | a Modern Guide to Traditional Native American Herbal Medicine. Herbalism Encyclopedia, Dispensatory, Recipes and Remedies for Everyday Health*. Independently Published.

Wuti Amadahy. (2021). *Native American Herbalism Encyclopedia: Traditional Herbal Remedies and Recipes to Heal Common Ailments*. Independently Published.

Exclusive Bonuses

Dear Reader,

I am thrilled to present to you a series of enriching bonuses that complement and enhance the themes explored in our exploration of Native American traditions and herbal wisdom in *"Lost Native American Herbalist's Secrets [All-In-1]."* These carefully curated resources are designed to deepen your understanding and connection to these ancient practices.

- **Bonus 1 - Sacred Roots: A Journal of Native American Herbal Traditions and Healing Practices:** This journal is a treasure trove of knowledge and insight. It offers a profound exploration of Native American herbal traditions, providing a space for you to record your own experiences and reflections as you journey through the world of healing herbs.
- **Bonus 2 - Green Harmony: The Essential Herb Garden Planner & Organizer:** This planner is an invaluable tool for anyone looking to cultivate their own herb garden. It provides guidance on plant selection, garden design, and maintenance, all while emphasizing the significance of harmony with nature, a principle deeply rooted in Native American culture.

- **Bonus 3 - Guided Herbal Meditation Script:** Journey Through the Healing Garden: Experience a unique meditative journey with this script. It guides you through a visualization of a healing garden, allowing you to connect spiritually with the natural world and the healing powers of herbs, embodying the essence of Native American herbal wisdom.

- **Bonus 4 - Nature's Gifts: A Glossary of 40 Essential Herbs in Native American Healing:** This glossary is a comprehensive guide to forty of the most revered herbs in Native American herbal medicine. It offers detailed descriptions, uses, and historical context, providing an invaluable resource for anyone interested in the healing power of nature.

- **Bonus 5 - Legends of Healing Plants: Native American Traditions:** Delve into the rich stories and legends surrounding Native American healing plants. This collection not only shares the cultural significance of various plants but also offers a glimpse into the spiritual and historical aspects of Native American traditions.

How to Access Your Bonuses:

Scan the QR Code Below: Simply use your phone's camera or a QR code reader to scan the code, and you'll be directly taken to the bonus content.

SCAN ME

Visit the Link: Alternatively, access these valuable resources by visiting our dedicated link. https://bit.ly/Amara-NAH

I hope these bonuses will enrich your journey into the world of Native American herbalism and traditions. May they inspire and guide you as you explore the ancient wisdom and practices that have nurtured and healed generations.

Warm regards,

Wilhelmina Amara

Made in the USA
Monee, IL
03 December 2024

72164689R00077